The American, Haitian, and Spanish American Revolutions 1775–1825

Social or Political?

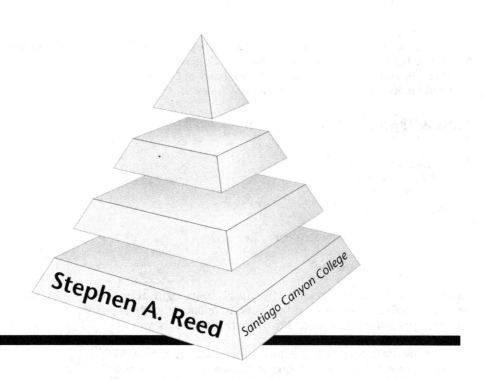

Stephen A. Reed   Santiago Canyon College

Kendall Hunt
publishing company

Cover images:
    Map of Haiti: Image copyright Martine Oger, 2008. Used under license from Shutterstock, Inc.
    Boston Tea Party image courtesy Library of Congress.
    Maximilian Robespierre image courtesy Library of Congress.
    Simón Bolívar image courtesy Library of Congress.

Kendall Hunt
publishing company

www.kendallhunt.com
Send all inquiries to:
4050 Westmark Drive
Dubuque, IA 52004-1840

Copyright © 2009, 2010 by Stephen A. Reed

ISBN 978-0-7575-7261-6

Printed in the United States of America
10 9 8 7 6 5 4 3 2

Dedication

To my muses: Rosie, Natalie, and Clio

Contents

Chapter Three   69

The Haitian Revolution: The Forgotten, Bloody, and Cautionary Revolution

Chapter Four   99

The Spanish American Revolutions: Inspired by the United States and France, Tempered by Haiti

Conclusion   133

Four Revolutions Compared

Introduction

Reflections from Teaching:
The Amazing Half Century 1775 to 1825

This book is intended for college students and the general reader who wish to gain an understanding of the first great age of revolutions. It is intended as an interpretative analysis of four revolutions that occurred in only fifty years—from approximately 1775 to 1825. It is not intended as a work of original research but rather as an expansion of a theoretical framework I have used in teaching my classes for many years, explaining the interrelationships, significances, and differences of four remarkable revolutions. I hope that the reader will find my framework useful and that it will provoke discussion.

During many years of teaching United States, Latin American, and world history, I was always struck by the amazing energy loosed by the American Revolution, how the French Revolution quickly followed and exceeded the American, how many have missed the pivotal importance of the Haitian Revolution, and how the Spanish American Revolution for independence completed the circle by making a revolution similar to the American. Also striking is how these four revolutions came in essentially two different varieties, two being primarily political revolutions and two definitely social revolutions.

Why Differentiate Types of Revolutions?

To divide revolutions between social and political varieties is obviously to make artificial distinctions, as revolutions are combinations of both types of changes. Nevertheless, these four revolutions clearly divide themselves into two general types, and the distinction of political or social is useful in seeing how fundamentally these revolutions vary.

The Concept of the Social Pyramid
What Constitutes a Social Revolution?
What Is a Political Revolution?

To demonstrate the difference between social and political revolutions, I have provided graphics showing the "social pyramid" before each revolution and how it was altered immediately after the revolution. Social and political power in all four revolutions can best be visualized in the form of a pyramid with a single person, or a small percentage of people, at the top of the power structure and large masses of people, essentially powerless, at the bottom. For the purposes of this interpretation, I define a political revolution as one in which one man, or relatively small group, is displaced by a different elite group, leaving the vast majority of people in the country in their original position of powerlessness. A social revolution, by contrast, topples the top of the pyramid and places a large swatch of the underclass in power. Using this definition, I contend that the American and Spanish American revolutions were political revolutions and that the French and Haitian revolutions were clearly social in nature.

The Four Revolutions Mutually Influence Each Other and History

The American Revolution began the great experiment in self-determination and self-government by the people. The French Revolution, the next in the series, was inspired by the American Revolution and, in turn, had a major impact on early American politics, including the development of the political party system. The French Revolution could not help but affect the French colonies, including Haiti (St. Dominique). While the French did not intend to extend liberty, equality, and fraternity to Haiti, the upheaval in France set in motion the only successful rebellion by a slave colony against a colonial power in history. The Haitian Revolution has been ignored by historians for reasons that will be discussed in this text, but it should not be. Among other results of the Haitian Revolution were the United States' acquisition of the Louisiana Purchase, the intensification of the slave system in the United States, and the determination of the Spanish American Creole leaders to make their independence from Spain a political rather than a social revolution.

The concept of people in a country controlling their own affairs through self-government was revolutionary in world history. The only other experiment in democracy occurred in ancient Greece, in Athens and a few other city-states, and only lasted about a hundred years. The question of whether an entire country, not just a city, could be governed under a democratic republican system worried the American founding fathers. They were also cognizant of the fact that in Athens, the birthplace of democracy, almost half of the population was excluded from governing the country due to their slave status (not to mention that women were excluded due to misogyny).

The extraordinary explosion of intellectual activity and the worldview of the Age of Enlightenment were primary sparks that greatly influenced all four revolutions. The men of the Enlightenment were optimistic. They believed that human beings were rational and that the world operated subject to a set of "natural laws" that men could understand. Whatever was rational was good, according to this set of concepts. What was definitely not logical was monarchy. The idea that just because a person survived his or her father to become a monarch seemed irrational. The new king might not have any administrative abilities, might in fact be an imbecile—which could, and did, happen under the system of hereditary monarchy. Thus, monarchical rule was irrational and bad.

The ideas of the French philosophers, men such as Rousseau, Voltaire, and Montesquieu, were read by leaders of all four revolutions. This is all the more astounding in Catholic countries, such as France, Haiti, and Spanish America, where these books were often on an index of books forbidden by the Catholic Church. Yet, even Catholic priests, such as Father Hidalgo in México, had such books in their libraries. The American revolutionaries were particularly fond of the writings of John Locke. Large parts of the Declaration of Independence are lifted directly out of Locke's writings, including the assertion that "government rests upon the consent of the governed" and the idea that all men have "inalienable rights."

In addition to being devotees of the ideas of the Enlightenment, the revolutionaries had other allegiances in common. Many were Freemasons and/or deists. The importance of freemasonry in the revolutions is remarkable. Most of leaders of American independence, including George Washington and Benjamin Franklin, were Freemasons. Even more amazing, leaders of the South American revolutions, including San Martín and Bolívar, were Masons. This is all the more extraordinary, since the Catholic Church was opposed to freemasonry. Yet many of the leaders of the revolutions in Spanish America were Masons *and* believers in Catholic theology. They tended to be anti-clerical, opposed to the power of the church, but not its spiritual teachings. Masonry was also influential in France, but the ex-slaves who made the Haitian Revolution did not, at first, have the opportunity to become Masons.

Freemasonry was a secret, male fraternity. To become a Mason, a person had to believe in a "higher power," not necessarily the standard Christian god. Despite its elaborate initiation practices, Masons were rationalists. One of the concepts they considered most irrational was monarchy. Masonic lodges served as secret cells during the revolutionary age and continued to influence the politics of postrevolutionary governments. In fact, in early independent México, Liberal Party members tended to be York Rite Masons, and Conservative Party members were Scottish Rite Masons.

Deism, with its view of god as a "watchmaker" who created the world as a great clock and then let it operate according to "natural laws," was particularly important in the American Revolution. The deist god did not work in "mysterious ways" but rather invented a logical universe that operated in an understandable and predictable manner. This god did not perform miracles, and believers did not have a personal relationship with him. Americans often hear today that "America was founded as a Christian nation." That is true as far as it goes, but it does not go far enough. Yes, America was primarily Christian (there were a few Jews in colonial America), but many of our founding fathers were a particular type of Christian—deists—who don't exist today.

A word about women in this revolutionary era may be useful at this point. It's wonderful that the English language is flexible and that the word *mankind* can cover males and females as well. However, in the vast majority of cases, when the men of the Enlightenment wrote about the rights of men, they meant *men,* and not women. One of the most important documents created by the French Revolution was the *Declaration of the Rights of Man and the Citizen.* Although a parallel document was issued by a group of women declaring the rights of their gender, it was little noticed at the time. Though many women played prominent roles in all four revolutions, the postrevolutionary countries they created were still male dominated. For the most part, women would have to wait until well into the twentieth century to receive many civil rights, including the right to vote. The First Age of Revolutions did not create female equality with men.

Eminent historians have disagreed as to whether the American Revolution was a political or social revolution. Gordon Wood in *The Radicalism of the American Revolution* extends his analysis well into the 1840s to make the case that it was a social revolution. In this study I have concentrated on the period immediately after the revolutions occurred. I tend to agree more with Bernard Bailyn, who in his aptly named study *A Struggle for Power,* stresses that in the American Revolution the power of the British crown was replaced by that of American aristocrats (Washington, Jefferson, and John Adams, for example). My contention is that had the American Revolution been a true social revolution, someone from the middle or lower classes, such as Sam Adams, might have emerged into power.

There can be no doubt that the French Revolution was a social revolution. The king of France and thousands of nobles literally lost their heads in the upheaval. The power of the Catholic Church and the land-owning base of the nobles was destroyed forever. Despite an attempt at counterrevolution by the conservative powers of Europe, the King of France would never again rule in an absolute manner and the power of the church and the nobles could never be fully restored.

The Haitian Revolution, unjustly neglected by historians, is the only example of a slave colony throwing off its European master by force. The French masters in Haiti and their families were slaughtered by the pent-up fury of the abused slave population. This was a thoroughgoing social revolution that put the mulattoes and blacks in control of Haiti for good. It was such a thorough smashing of the ruling class that it seared into the consciousness of the slave owners in the United States and resolved the ruling class in Spanish America to never allow their independence from Spain to become a social revolution.

The Spanish American aristocrats, or Creoles (*criollos* in Spanish), as Spaniards born in America were not as concerned with the uprising of black slaves as they were with the potential for an Indian revolt. Indians constituted the large underclass in Spanish America and had engaged in numerous revolts against the Spanish authorities over the years. That black slavery was relatively less economically important in mainland Spanish America than in the United States or the Caribbean is attested to by the fact that most of the newly formed republics quickly outlawed slavery. In the United States, of course, it took a civil war to end the curse of slavery.

The Spanish American Revolution for independence brings the first age of revolutions full circle. The American Revolution inspired the French to attempt to end the absolute rule of kings. However, the French Revolution quickly morphed from an attempt to bring about liberty, equality, and fraternity into a bloody social revolution. Even the most liberal Frenchman never intended for Saint Dominique (Haiti) to have a similar bloody revolution, which would topple the rule of the French. The excesses of the Haitian Revolution convinced the Creoles of Spanish America to construct a political revolution like that of the United States and not one that would cause them to lose their power—or their lives.

Only in México did Father Hidalgo's abortive uprising of mestizos and Indians portend a social upheaval, and it was quickly snuffed out. Although blacks and Indians fought in the Spanish American revolutions for independence (on both the royalist and patriot sides), they did not emerge into power immediately after Spanish American independence. Thus, the Spanish American revolutions were political in nature, with the creoles replacing the king of Spain and peninsular-born Spaniards in power.

The Spanish American aristocrats, although they attempted to adopt U.S.-style constitutions, were unable to make them work in the early nineteenth century. As we shall see in the following discussions of the Spanish and British colonial systems, the Spanish Americans did not have the requisite experience to make a democratic system work, while the British Americans, fortunate enough to be under the loose control of England, did gain such experience. It is remarkable that so many years after the United States embarked on its democratic experiment, American revolutionary ideals can still inspire. Consider the example of Chinese students in Tiananmen Square passing out copies of the Declaration of Independence and constructing a model of the Statue of Liberty.

The phrase *First Age of Revolutions* implies that there must be later ages of revolutions. Indeed there have been further revolutions after this first great age. The revolutions that occurred in Europe in 1848 were largely abortive. But in 1910, one of the major upheavals in world history occurred—the Mexican Revolution. Active warfare in México continued for ten years. While the Mexican Revolution was in process, another great revolution, the Russian, occurred in 1917. Together with the Chinese Communist Revolution of 1949 and the Cuban Revolution of 1959, these revolutions constitute a Second Age of Revolutions. A similar "compare and contrast" evaluation of these later revolutions may be instructive but is outside the scope of this book.

As we embark on our journey through the First Age of Revolutions, I invite the reader to share with me the exhilaration and awe inspired by the spectacle of men attempting to throw off the fetters of the past and attempting to construct societies dedicated to self-determination and the realization of full human potential. That the men of this age did not always succeed in accomplishing the just societies they sought in no way detracts from their valiant efforts to achieve them.

The American Revolution

1

The First and Inspirational Revolution

The Social Pyramid before the American Revolution

King of England

American Aristocrats (Washington, Jefferson, John Adams)

Lower/Middle Classes (Sam Adams)

(White Women)

Black Slaves/Indians

▲ A Comparison of the Spanish and British Colonies

Although the American Revolution is the first in the series of revolutions to occur between 1775 and 1825, the English empire was not the first European empire in America. The English were, in fact, "Johnnies-come-lately." The first empire was that of the Spanish. Columbus projected Spanish power into the Western Hemisphere during his epic voyage of 1492. The first permanent Spanish colony in the New World was established on the Caribbean island the Spanish called Hispaniola in 1496. In contrast, the first permanent English colony in the New World was Jamestown, Virginia, founded in 1607.

The Spanish colonies are therefore the proper yardstick for comparison with the English colonies. There were both similarities and differences between the Spanish colonies and the English colonies in America. In fact, in many ways, the English attempted to copy the Spanish successes.

However, the English were never able to emulate the Spanish in two major ways, no matter how hard they tried. The first difference was that the Spanish found a great deal of mineral wealth, gold and silver, in Central and South America. Englishmen spent a great deal of time searching for equivalent wealth in North America, to no avail. Some of the early English gentlemen who attempted to colonize in the North Carolina area would have been far better off spending their initial efforts planting crops rather than hunting for gold.

The other major difference between the Spanish and English colonies has to do with the number and types of "Indians" found in the respective empires. Of course, the people Columbus called "Indians" were not Indians at all, since they did not live in India, but were rather indigenous peoples who had originally migrated to the Americas over a land bridge then existing between Siberia and Alaska about 30,000 years before Columbus's arrival. Columbus hopefully, and mistakenly, called them Indians under the impression that he had reached his original destination, Asia. Columbus's concept of sailing west to get east was a correct one, since the world is spherical. Unfortunately, Columbus also underestimated the size of the earth by one third, not realizing that another two continents existed between Europe and Asia! Despite a great deal of evidence to the contrary, Columbus continued to hope and even state that he believed he had reached Asia. That doubts had begun to creep into Columbus's mind is evidenced by an incident that apparently occurred during a voyage around the island of Cuba, when Columbus had his sailors swear they believed they had reached the orient.

Whereas the Spanish encountered millions of sedentary Indians in the Aztec, Maya, and Inca empires, the English found a much smaller number of Indians in their empire. For the most part these Indians were not sedentary but rather mainly hunter-gatherers who moved around a great deal. The significance of this difference is that the Spanish were able to effectively use the large sedentary populations of Aztecs, Maya, and Incas as a workforce, whereas the English were largely unsuccessful at putting "their" Indians to work.

Spain rapidly became a wealthy nation based on the large amounts of gold and silver mined in México and Perú. In contrast, when the English began their colonization of America, they were a relatively poorer country and this forced them to rely more on individual enterprise, rather than state sponsorship, for their initial attempts at settling in North America.

From the very first Spanish voyage, Spanish expeditions to America were funded by the Spanish crown. Early English colonization, on the other hand, depended on private enterprise or joint stock companies rather than direct funding from the English crown. This difference carried great ramifications for the respective degrees of control over their colonies between the English and Spanish colonies. From the start, Spain exercised a great deal more control over their colonies than the English did over theirs.

Both the Spanish and the English believed in an economic concept called *mercantilism.* Under this concept, colonies exist basically for the benefit of the mother country. Colonies were only to trade with the mother country (or other fellow Spanish and British colonies) and with no other nation. Also, the colonies were limited under the mercantilist system as to the type of goods they could produce. Colonies were primarily to produce raw materials to be sent to the mother country. The mother country would then send manufactured goods back to the colonies. These trade regulations often became downright absurd. For example, the English colonies were allowed to produce beaver pelts but not beaver hats. The hats had to be made in England and shipped back to America. Remember, that from the standpoint of the Europeans, their colonies existed for the sole purpose of enriching the mother country. The belief at the time was that a country's wealth was measured in gold and silver, and by this definition, the English colonies failed, while the Spanish succeeded.

To make up for their lack of mineral wealth, the English attempted to establish their empire "on the cheap." First they entrusted early colonization efforts to private entrepreneurs like Sir Walter Raleigh. When Raleigh's several efforts to found a colony in the area of North Carolina failed, it was revealed that such colonization was beyond the means of a single individual. The English monarchs then turned to granting colonies to joint stock companies. Such companies were the forerunners of the modern corporation, in which individuals bought stock in the colonization

King James I
He was not in favor of tobacco.
(Library of Congress)

company and shared in the profits, or losses, of the colony in proportion to the amount of capital they invested. This was a thrifty arrangement for the English crown, which did not have to put up its own funds.

The first permanent English colony, Jamestown, Virginia, was founded by the Virginia Company in 1607. It would take a number of years for Virginians to find a product with which to make money before they would give up the quest for gold. That product was tobacco. It would not be a great exaggeration to state that the country that eventually became the United States was founded on tobacco. Columbus had observed Indians smoking tobacco in the Caribbean. Indians generally only smoked tobacco on ceremonial occasions—unlike modern tobacco fiends who light the next cigarette from the butt of the last one. Tobacco was a profitable product for Virginians precisely because it was addictive!

One person who was not a fan of tobacco was King James I, who wrote:

> Smoking tobacco is loathsome to the nose, harmful to the brain, dangerous to the lungs, and the black stinking fume thereof, nearest resembling the horrible Stygian smoke of the pit [hell] that is bottomless.

> *Workes of King James of 1616,* 1905 Reprint by G. Putnam & Sons, London.

Nevertheless, once tobacco reached Europe, the North Americans found a reliable, addicted, and productive market for their product. The conflicted relationship with tobacco in the United States today can been seen in two opposing facts: the government advises Americans not to smoke, while simultaneously subsidizing tobacco farmers.

From the very beginning, the Spanish empire was ruled "top down," with all instructions and laws for the colonies originating in Spain. Shortly after the founding of Santo Domingo, the Spanish established the Casa de Contratacíon, which administered all aspects of trade and navigation between Spain and its American colonies. It took the English until 1696 to set up a similar institution, the Board of

Trade and Plantations, and its powers were not nearly as sweeping as those of the Casa de Contratacíon.

British Colonization: Inconsistent, Indulgent, and Created on the Cheap

From early on, the English often left the colonies to their own devices. Smuggling and trading with unauthorized countries were American traditions. The English attempted to codify their restrictive mercantilist rules of trade in the Navigation Acts. These acts, enacted by the mother country between 1660 and 1672, spelled out the ideal of how colonial trade was supposed to work. As we shall see, the English were wildly inconsistent in the application of these trade restrictions.

The Navigation Acts imposed three main requirements. The first was that all trade between England and the colonies must be carried in ships built, owned, and manned by British subjects. For purposes of this requirement, Americans were, of course, British subjects. Secondly, all European goods imported into the colonies must pass through England first. If the colonists wished to important goods from France, for example, by law the French goods had to pass through England first. Of course, the British middlemen then took their cut of the profits, increasing the cost of these goods to the Americans. Finally, certain "enumerated goods"—products produced by the colonies—could only be shipped to Britain, or British colonies. This was true even if they were ultimately destined for other European countries. Tobacco was the first product to be "enumerated," but by the Revolution, virtually every product of the American colonies was on the enumerated list.

The Navigation Acts were not completely negative in their economic impact on colonists. Americans received a monopoly of the tobacco trade in England. Also, the exclusion of foreign ships was a boost to the ship building industry in New England. Still, American colonials had no desire to have their choice of trading partners circumscribed by the mother country. Fortunately for the Americans, their masters in England spent large stretches of time not enforcing the Navigation Acts.

The author of the policy of not enforcing the Navigation Acts was Sir Robert Walpole. Walpole became the king's chief minister in 1721. His policy of "salutary neglect" reasoned that since the English economy and the American economies were in a healthy state, even though the Americans were ignoring the rules and smuggling, it was better to ignore those transgressions than to risk undermining the prosperous status quo. Thus, turning a blind eye to American violations of the Navigation Acts was "salutary," or healthy, since everyone was making hefty profits.

Sir Robert Walpole
Author of the policy of "salutary neglect"
(Library of Congress)

Walpole followed this policy from 1721 to 1742, and it was carried on by his successors well into the 1760s. Note that this policy of tolerating smuggling was carried on until less than twenty years before the American Revolution. No wonder the Americans reacted so violently when English policy began to try to enforce the trading laws after so long a period of nonenforcement.

To illustrate the differences between England's administration of its colonies and Spain's view of its, consider the analogy of two school teachers. The first teacher is very strict. The first time a student acts up in class, he gives him a rap on the knuckles or sends him to the principal's office. The strict teacher represents the Spanish viewpoint on how to deal with the colonies. The other teacher takes a laid-back, hands-off approach to the classroom. Soon the students are taking all kinds of liberties in class, talking when they should be listening and disobeying the teacher. Finally, when this teacher has had enough, he suddenly tries to impose order—and has a much harder time than the teacher who was strict from the beginning. The inconsistent teacher represents the English approach to its empire. Trade policy is but one example of inconsistent English administration.

To illustrate the American tradition of smuggling, we turn to what historians usually call the *triangular trade*. There were many different versions. One was for New Englanders to take colonial raw materials such as wheat, fish, and fruit to the Caribbean. These products would be exchanged for molasses. Molasses is the result of reducing sugar cane to thick syrup. According to the Navigation Acts, the colonists were only supposed to trade with the British West Indian Colonies. But being sharp Yankee traders, they purchased their molasses wherever they could get the best deal, including French and Spanish colonies. The molasses was then taken back to New England where it was refined into rum.

Rum was then shipped to Africa. It was supposed to go through England first, but the Americans rarely fulfilled this requirement of the Navigation Acts. They once again disobeyed the rules, thus avoiding the English middleman's cut. The rum was then exchanged for slaves and the slaves traded in the Caribbean for molasses as the triangle continued.

Why didn't the Americans sell the slaves in North Carolina or Virginia instead of in the Caribbean? The answer is surprising in view of the economic realities of the twenty-first century. At that time, small Caribbean islands like Jamaica, Barbados, and Santo Domingo (Haiti) were fabulously wealthy sources of income for European colonial powers. Today, of course, these islands are much poorer than the United States. But during colonial times the reverse was true. Thus, Americans could make a great deal more money by selling slaves in the Caribbean than they could in North America. The value of these small islands at the time is best illustrated by the fact that England, after winning the French and Indian Wars, actually considered taking the small island of Guadeloupe rather than Canada as compensation. The British also reasoned that a French Canada would cause the Americans to want to stay in the British Empire, to retain the "protection" of the English against the French. In the end, however, land hunger triumphed and the English seized Canada, eliminating the French threat to the American colonists.

Another way in which the English colonies differed from the Spanish colonies was in the amount of self-governance each permitted. The highest position allowed to the Creoles, or Spaniards born in America, was to be a member of the town council *(cabildo)*. Spanish laws for the colonies all originated in Spain. The Americans, by contrast, were writing many of their own laws since the founding of the House of Burgesses in 1619. By the time of the American Revolution, all thirteen colonies had legislatures and were writing their own laws. Thus by the time of the Revolution, Americans had more than 150 years of experience as legislators. This helps to explain why the Americans were able to create and perpetuate a successful democratic-republican form of government. Despite the fact that many Latin American countries admired the United States' form of government—and in fact often adopted constitutions that were virtually copies of the American constitution—they could not make the democratic system work until well into the twentieth century. This is due to the fact that the American aristocrats had vast experience in self-government and the Spanish American aristocrats did not.

A prime example of the English tendency to try to run the colonies cheaply was how the colonial governors were compensated. Colonial governors were appointed by the king and sent to America with instructions issued by the Board of Trade. The governor had an absolute veto over legislation passed by the colonial assemblies. While the governor seemed to have dictatorial power over the assemblies, most governors chose cooperation with the assemblies rather than confrontation. There was a simple economic explanation for this. In a desire to administer America in the thriftiest possible way, the crown allowed the colonists to pay the governor. Thus, if the governors wanted to get paid, and most did, they went along with the legislation passed by the colonial assemblies.

The structure of the American colonial governments can be visualized as the forerunner of the present presidential/congressional relationship. Under the governor was a governor's council appointed by the king. Below that was an elected assembly. The structure looked like this:

Governor
Governor's Council
Assembly

The council and the assembly functioned something like a bicameral legislature, similar to today's House of Representatives and Senate. A critical question for the analysis of whether the American Revolution was a social or political revolution is who were these men who served in the governor's councils and assemblies?

▲ The Colonial Social Pyramid

The council members were American aristocrats. In the free enterprise society of the American colonies, some capitalists were more successful than others. Successful tobacco planters, for example, soon acquired more land and slaves. By the late seventeenth century, the successful planters were driving their rivals out of business. Likewise, the more prosperous merchants and professional men emerged as an elite class in the towns. The British government encouraged the growth of this American aristocracy. It paralleled the English aristocracy at home. The crown felt that it could work with such men and thus appointed them to positions of political influence, such as the governor's council.

The method of selecting men for the colonial assemblies varied by time and location. By the late seventeenth century, property qualifications restricted the number of white men who could vote. For instance, in some colonies a voter had to own fifty acres of land, or a lot in a town. Though land owning was common in the colonies. More than half the men in New York, for instance, were disenfranchised by such a requirement. When we consider that women, Indians, and black slaves were barred from voting, the men who owned property and served in the assemblies and governor's councils definitely constituted an elite. This elite would lead the American Revolution and take up power after the success of that revolution.

The Social Pyramid and Race

Both the English and Spanish colonies enslaved Africans. However, black slavery was much more economically important in the English colonies than in the Spanish. The reason for this goes back to the fact that the Spanish colonies had large sedentary populations of Indians. Although Indians were not slaves under Spanish law, they constituted the major portion of the workforce in Spanish America and often worked under slavelike conditions. Since large numbers of Indians were available to the Spanish, black slavery was of secondary importance. This is reflected in the fact that the Spanish American countries abolished slavery shortly after independence, while the abolition of slavery in the United States required a civil war.

In 1619—ironically the same year as the founding of the House of Burgesses—the first cargo of African slaves appeared in Virginia. The contrast between the founding of the first legislative body in the English colonies and the arrival of slaves is striking. The inherent contradiction between the beginnings of a system of individual freedom in America and the founding of the slave system became a balancing act for statesmen. This contradiction would bedevil the early United States and culminate in a bloody civil war.

The first slaves introduced into the English colonies were brought by a Dutch ship. However, it could well have been a ship from another European country. Virtually all Europeans were involved in the slave trade at the time. On the African side of the slave trade, native Africans were selling slaves to the Europeans. There was plenty of blame to go around in the slave trade.

Nor was slavery rare in the history of man. Nearly all the ancient civilizations practiced slavery: the Mesopotamians, Egyptians, Chinese, and Indus civilizations. However, there was a major difference between slavery in earlier civilizations and that practiced in the Americas. Slavery in earlier civilizations was a matter of personal misfortune. Slaves were either captured in battle, became slaves because of debt or commission of a crime, or sold themselves into slavery. Earlier slavery was not based on skin color. The tragedy of American slavery was that it was tied to skin color. This would have momentous implications for the abolishment of slavery and future race relations in the United States.

Nothing in Virginia law in 1619 defined a permanent, lifelong slavery status for the Africans who were sold to the Virginians. The concept that Africans were slaves and that their children were likewise slaves for life evolved over time. Slaves might instead have been treated as indentured servants. Because passage to America was so expensive, a large percentage of colonists came to the New World as indentured servants, with their passage paid for by a master. Once they served their "indenture" by working for their masters for five to seven years, they became free to seek their own fortunes. Often indentured servants would "run away" to avoid serving their full period of indenture. English indentured servants who did this easily blended into the general population. Alas, there was no such escape for African slaves, whose skin color gave them away. Africans forcibly ripped away from their homes and cultures had little defense in the New World against their masters.

Unfortunately, whenever one human being has absolute control over another, great abuses occur, up to and including rape. Slave masters quickly took advantage of slave women with the inevitable result that children were born from these pairings. Then the question of how these children would rank in society became acute. The decision was that children of the slave master and slave women would be treated as slaves and not acknowledged as the master's children.

A unique definition of who was "black" arose in what would become the United States. In virtually every other country there is a separate racial classification for the offspring of a white person and a black person. In most of Latin America that classification is *mulatto*. Even in South Africa during apartheid, there was a separate classification for mixed-race persons. This tragedy of American slavery has lived on as racism.

Race is not a scientific fact but rather a social construct. There is only one race, the human race. The belief in race is what the English author Ashley Montagu called in his aptly titled book *Man's Most Dangerous Myth*. Nevertheless, it is important because people believe there is such a thing as race—and therefore they are willing to perpetuate all kinds of atrocities in the name of it.

Barack Obama is no more black than he is white; his father was black and his mother was white. Tiger Woods is no more black than he is Asian, for the same reason. Homer Plessy, the man whose case went all the way to the Supreme Court in *Plessy v. Ferguson* was only one-eighth black. Nevertheless, the court used this case in 1896 to rule that segregation was constitutional—and by implication that an American with even one drop of black blood could face legal discrimination. The Supreme Court did not correct this egregious error until the *Brown v. Board of Education* decision in 1954. Miscegenation laws, which outlawed the marriage of people of different races, were widespread in the United States. To use Virginia as an example, it was illegal for a white person and black person to marry until the case of *Loving v. Virginia* struck down miscegenation laws in 1960. There are grounds for Americans to be optimistic about the future of race relations in this country, since I would maintain that the country is a far different place than it was in 1954—only a little more than fifty years ago, which is the blink of an eye in historical time. What best illustrates that the American Revolution was not a social revolution in terms of race is that slavery continued after the revolution. Under the Constitution, slaves were to be counted as three-fifths of a person, which is a sad commentary in itself.

Contrary to popular belief, slavery originally existed in all thirteen colonies. The difference between the North and the South was that slavery was much more economically important in the South; thus, while northern colonies eventually outlawed slavery, the South never did. A civil war finally freed the United States from slavery.

The English and Spanish empires were also different in their view of the Indians. When Columbus arrived in the New World, he enslaved the Indians. But champions of the Indians soon appeared, such as the priest Bartolomé de Las Casas. Las Casas successfully argued before Queen Isabela that Indians could not be enslaved since they were *"gente de razon"* (people of reason) who could understand the Christian faith. When Las Casas's opponents demanded to know who worked for the Spanish, he answered in a moment of weakness that Africans could be imported to do the work in the Spanish colonies. Las Casas later recanted this suggestion and stated that black slavery was wrong "for the same reason."

The fact that the Spanish considered the Indians people of reason who could not be enslaved and who were candidates for conversion to Catholicism is highly significant as conversion of the Indians soon became a prime goal of Spanish colonization and an official governmental policy. The English crown never made the conversion of Indians a policy. This difference is interesting since the "Black Legend" portrayed the Spanish as uniquely cruel towards the Indians—more cruel than any other European empire in America. This "Black Legend" is truly a legend that has more to do with dynastic and religious rivalries than any poorer treatment of Indians by one group of Europeans over another.

The best way to view the English thinking about the Indians is that they were an "obstacle." To the English, the Indians were not "using" the land, which is to say they were not chopping down trees and building cities. This reflects a major cultural misunderstanding. Indians in North and South America did not believe that anyone could personally own land. Rather, they believed that the land belonged to all in common. The fact that Europeans and Indians were divided by a vast cultural gulf is best illustrated by the apocryphal story of the Dutch "purchase" of Manhattan Island. (An *apocryphal story* is one that probably never happened but nevertheless illustrates an important point.) The story is that the Dutch purchased Manhattan Island for twenty-four dollars worth of glass beads. The Dutch thought the Indians foolish for selling a whole island for such a trifle. The Indians thought the Dutch crazy because "everyone knew" that land could not be privately owned, so they were happy to accept the beads. The joke may have been on both groups, since the Indians who sold the island might not even have lived there!

Neither the American Revolution nor the later Spanish American revolutions elevated the status of the Indian. In fact, Indians, the very first Americans, did not become U.S. citizens until the 1880s under the Dawes Act. Even then, Indians could not become American citizens unless they lived in nontribal fashion. One Indian chief testifying before Congress only partly sarcastically stated that the White Man should put Indians on wheels—so he could move them about more easily.

The Importance of Religious Freedom

Religious freedom was a major motivation for immigration to what became the United States. This is in contrast to the Spanish colonists, who were overwhelmingly Catholic. Immigrants to what would become the United States were diverse in their religious beliefs, espousing not only Catholicism but many flavors of Protestantism and even Judaism. Spanish colonialism began before the Protestant Reformation, while the first permanent colony in British North America was founded after the Reformation was well underway.

Martin Luther, a Catholic monk, had launched the Reformation in Germany in 1517 with his Ninety-five Theses. These were ninety-five objections Luther raised about the Catholic Church. This marked the beginning of the Protestant movement (there were also aspects of German nationalism in Luther's movement). Protestantism of various forms quickly spread in Europe, and the Catholic Church launched a Counter-Reformation in response.

The reformation made little headway in England before 1533. In that year King Henry VIII requested from the Pope an annulment of his marriage. The motive behind this request was that Henry's queen, Catherine of Aragon, had not produced a male heir to the throne. Henry believed that if he could marry another (younger) woman, he might have a son. It was not widely understood at the time that the man's contribution to conception determines the sex of the child. It was not unprecedented for the pope to annul royal marriages, not even long-standing unions such as Henry's.

Henry had some hope of success in receiving this annulment as he was well regarded by the Pope. He had been named "Defender of the Faith" by the Pope and written defenses of Catholicism. But the question of the annulment became entangled in European dynastic politics. Catherine's cousin Charles I of Spain was also Charles V of the Holy Roman Empire (Germany). Charles wished to protect Catherine's claim to the English throne. Charles also controlled much territory in Italy at the time. As a result and after much intrigue, Henry's annulment was denied.

Henry then decided that the Church in England would be headed by the King of England and not the Pope. The result was the Church of England (Anglican) Church. Little about the Church of England changed except who headed it. The liturgy continued to be essentially Catholic. Nevertheless, this was a step toward England eventually becoming a majority Protestant nation. Catholics and Protestants fought each other ferociously in England, and many people whose views were not favored at a particular time sought religious freedom in America.

Thus, the Spanish-English rivalry was not just a contest for empire. It became a religious contest and even a personal one, given Henry's rejection of his Spanish-born wife. The English were only too happy to play up the "Black Legend" of unique Spanish cruelty. Father Las Casas, defender of the Indians of America, unwittingly provided propaganda ammunition to the English by the publication of his book *Breve Relación*. This was an account of Spanish cruelties toward the Indians of the Caribbean, written to convince Queen Isabela to outlaw Indian slavery. The English picked up this book, translated it, and added vivid illustrations of Spanish barbarities to attack the Spanish in this colonial, religious, and personal squabble.

This is not a bad time to point out another major difference between the English and Spanish colonies. Very few Spanish women ever came to the New World, while a great number of English women did. Not only did English women come to the New World in great numbers, they also seem to have had an inordinately large number of offspring; eight or ten children per family were not unusual. Since the conquistadores suffered a shortage of Spanish women in America, they looked to Indian women for their female companionship. The children produced were something new in the world—*mestizos,* a mixture of Spanish and Indian genes. The Church in Spanish America soon moved to legitimize this process by marrying Spaniards and Indians. Likewise, in French Canada, a shortage of European women led to a similar close relationship between the French and Indian women.

Seeking freedom to practice their various religious beliefs, different groups tended to settle in different parts of British North America. Thus, Catholics tended to immigrate to Maryland when they were out of favor in the mother country. Maryland had been established by an English Catholic nobleman, George Calvert (Lord Baltimore), as a refuge for his coreligionists in America. Maryland, like Virginia, soon developed its own colonial legislature. The most notable law passed by this legislature was the Act of Toleration, which promised religious toleration to both Catholics and Protestants in Maryland. While this was not complete freedom of religion, it was a move in that direction and a welcome change from Europe, where Catholics often killed Protestants and Protestants killed Catholics.

Puritans, so called because they wished to "purify" (that is, make more Protestant) the Church of England, settled in New England. The most famous group of Puritans who set sail on the *Mayflower,* through an incredibly poor feat of navigation, landed not in Virginia, where they had been granted land, but in Massachusetts. The *Mayflower* voyage is so celebrated that it is fashionable, especially on the East Coast, to claim that one's ancestors came to this country on that vessel. That ship—a boat really—was not that large and if all the families that claim to have come over on it actually did, it would have sunk at the dock! Before they got off the boat, the Puritans wrote a remarkable document, the Mayflower Compact. The compact called for church government based on the idea of democracy as a guiding principle. Despite the fact that this was a religious, rather than a civil, document, it is seen by many historians as a step in the direction of democratic government.

It is not surprising that when the first democratic revolution occurred, it occurred in a British colony. The English monarchical system was in a sense the most liberal in the world. At least, it was liberal in the sense that the English king was limited in his powers, which he had to share with others. In comparison with the king of France and especially the czar of Russia, the English king was highly limited in his power. This limitation dates back to 1215, when King John was forced to share power with the nobles by being forced to sign the Magna Carta. The English Parliament asserted more and more power as time went on. The struggle between the Parliament and the king culminated in a civil war won by the parliamentary forces over which Charles I literally lost his head. When the English monarchy was restored, there was no question about the powers of Parliament. This was the tradition to which Americans added colonial legislatures and the Mayflower Compact.

In order for the future United States to avoid being torn apart, like the Old World, by religious conflict, there evolved a tradition of religious tolerance and separation of church and state. Roger Williams, whose radical ideas

Roger Williams
Pioneer of separation of church and state
(Library of Congress)

of religious freedom brought him into conflict with the Puritan authorities in Massa-chusetts, founded the colony of Rhode Island in 1644. Williams believed in com-plete freedom of worship and separation of church and state. He believed that state-established religions forced people to worship and that "forced worship stinks in God's nostrils." Therefore, no one in Rhode Island would be molested by the author-ities because of his religious convictions as long as he kept the civil peace. Not sur-prisingly, Rhode Island soon became a refuge for all sorts of religious free thinkers. For instance, Ann Hutchinson, who came into conflict with the Puritan authorities in Massachusetts, relocated to Rhode Island.

Ann Hutchinson had dared to debate theology with male church authorities. Her literacy points out another aspect that would aid Americans in their Revolution and administration of their new government—the large number of educated Americans, found especially in the Northern colonies. The Puritans, believing that all should be able to read the Bible, including women, had decreed that all towns of a certain size should have an elementary school, and larger towns even had secondary schools. The Puritan clergy in America were highly educated and included many graduates of Oxford and Cambridge. Harvard University, the first university in the North Ameri-can colonies, was established as an institution to train Puritan ministers.

Another religious minority persecuted in the Old World was the Society of Friends, commonly known as *Quakers,* because they were said to tremble, or quake, in God's sight. They believed that people needed to examine their consciences to discover their "inner light." One of the tenets of Quakerism is pacifism. The Friends were also the first religious group in the colonies to speak out against slavery and were instrumental in developing the Underground Railroad to help escaped slaves make their way to freedom.

William Penn was the son of a British admiral who was a friend of the Duke of York. In short, Penn was well situated in English society. However, he converted to Quakerism and was sent to prison for his religious beliefs. Penn dreamed of a home-land in the New World for Quakers and other religious dissenters. The royal family, the Stuarts, owed Penn's father a large sum of money. This debt caused Charles II to grant to William Penn the territory that is now Pennsylvania in 1681.

Pennsylvania became a sanctuary in the New World, not only for Quakers but for other despised religious minorities in Europe, particularly German Mennonites and the Amish. There were soon so many Germans in Pennsylvania that the local population mistakenly referred to them as "Pennsylvania Dutch" because they spoke Deutsch, or German.

All of this religious diversity makes the American Revolution unique among the four revolutions we will consider. The French, Haitian, and Spanish American revolutions all took place in predominately Catholic countries. Although there were anti-clerical and even anti-religious aspects to the other three revolutions, the issue of religious diversity was most acute in the American Revolution. It is no wonder that the very first amendment to the United States Constitution deals with, among other freedoms, freedom to practice any religion and the freedom to have no religion. Those who wish to push their religious views on others in the United States would do well to reflect on the problems, including religious killings, that result in systems where there is an established religion and persecution of religious minorities and atheists. In fact, the American Revolution could never have succeeded if the patriots had not adopted an attitude of religious tolerance. They would have been too busy fighting religious wars to wage a war for independence.

The Impact of the French and Indian Wars

The immediate catalyst for the American Revolution was the French and Indian Wars and the English policies regarding trade and taxation arising in their wake. The French and Indian Wars were a series of wars fought in both America and Europe from 1689 to 1763. In America these wars are called King William's War, Queen Ann's War, King George's War, and the French and Indian War. In European history they have different names. In this chapter we are concerned with their effect on the American Revolution.

In the first three of four French and Indian Wars, the French and their Indian allies raided the New England and New York frontiers. It is important to note that Indians fought on both sides of these wars. The Hurons and Algonquins were allied with the French, and the Iroquois were allied with the British. In general, the French had better relations with the Indians than the British did. Due to the small number of Frenchmen in Canada, the French had to rely on cooperation with the Indians, since they could not overwhelm them with numbers. The ultimate importance of the French and Indian Wars in America was that they eliminated the French as competitors for the American colonists in North America. There was also fighting along the Georgia/Spanish Florida border, since the Spanish were allied with the French beginning with Queen Ann's War.

The only territorial change that resulted from the first three of these wars was that Nova Scotia, Newfoundland, and Hudson Bay went from French to British control. The major part of Canada was still in French hands.

During intervals of peace, the French had been moving south along the Mississippi River. In 1718 they founded New Orleans, which became a major threat to British interests in the New World. Even at this time, the British subjects, who would soon find self-identity as "Americans" were looking to the trans-Mississippi west as an area for expansion. (An aside about the term *American:* Properly speaking, everyone from Canada to the southern tip of South America is an American. But the United States soon expropriated this term as its own.) New Orleans dominated the whole Ohio–Mississippi River complex and whoever controlled New Orleans controlled all commerce that came down the river system. With the then-primitive road system, New Orleans was an absolute choke point for trade in the interior of North America. It is no wonder that future president Thomas Jefferson was so concerned to acquire New Orleans. As we shall see in later chapters, it was the Haitian Revolution that made this purchase possible.

The French and Indian Wars were the training grounds for future American military leaders. Thus, the English sent out a young Virginia militia commander, George Washington, to try to prevent the French from building a fort in the Ohio River valley. This was Fort Duquesne, which stood on the present site of Pittsburgh, Pennsylvania. Washington failed to destroy the French fort, but in this he did no worse than the English General James Braddock, who was also defeated by the French. Braddock's defeat opened the whole frontier to attack by the French and their Indian allies.

In defeat, Washington learned the art of proper retreat. He was a great "retreater." This may sound odd as a military attribute, but there are different types of retreats. An army may throw down its weapons and run like rabbits to be forever dispersed, or it may adhere to an orderly process to stay together and fight on another day. Washington would be called upon many times during the Revolution to successfully employ the art of retreat.

The French and Indian Wars turned in favor of the British when William Pitt took over as the Prime Minister. Pitt ordered a series of attacks against Canada, which ultimately ended in the capture of Quebec by General James Wolfe. Unfortunately for General Wolfe, he was mortally wounded in the assault on Quebec. Nevertheless, Wolfe's victory was the effective end of the French and Indians Wars.

William Pitt (The Elder), Prime Minister and author of the English victory in the French and Indian Wars
(Library of Congress)

In the Treaty of Paris of 1763, England gained Canada and Florida. Spain had been allied with France at the end of the French and Indian Wars. However, Florida would soon revert to Spain. New Orleans and Louisiana were transferred from France to Spain. The Americans were happy with this development because Spain was now much weaker militarily than France, and this promised to make it easier to detach New Orleans and the surrounding area from Spain than it would have been from France. Unfortunately for the Americans, due to European dynastic considerations, Louisiana soon landed back in the control of France. Napoleon would ultimately sell it to the United States due to his loss of Haiti caused by the successful slave rebellion in St. Dominique. As mentioned earlier, England considered taking the rich Caribbean island of Guadeloupe rather than Canada in compensation for its victory. By taking Canada instead, the English eliminated the French threat to the American colonies and thus removed a powerful reason for the Americans to stay in the British Empire.

The American colonists were thrilled by the English victory in the French and Indians Wars. They were proud to be Englishmen, and they thought of their rights and liberties as English rights and liberties. Many Americans, including the future first President George Washington, fought in these wars, side-by-side with the British. But in only a dozen years, they would be shooting at the English and demanding their independence. How did this radical change in American thinking occur in such a short time? The roots of the American rebellion lay in the removal of the French threat, the British tradition of a limited monarchy, the liberal ideals of the Enlightenment, and above all, the inconsistency of English policies of trade and governance toward the colonies.

The Roots of Revolution

The American Revolution was a triumph of the liberal ideals of the Enlightenment. It was no coincidence that it succeeded against the most limited system of monarchy in Europe. The Glorious Revolution of 1688–1689 overthrew the Catholic King James II and replaced him with William of Orange and the Protestant daughter of James, Mary (William and Mary).

The Glorious Revolution established an English Bill of Rights and further limited the monarch's powers. The king or queen of England could not suspend laws of Parliament, levy taxes, make appointments, or maintain an army with the consent of Parliament. The American colonists thought of the colonial assemblies as their version of Parliament. Because the Americans had no representatives in the British Parliament and because they had been making their own laws since 1619, they quickly jumped to the concept that they could only be taxed by their own representatives. This was later to be immortalized in the famous formulation, "no taxation without representation."

The American aristocrats who would soon lead the Revolution had wide access to the writings of the French and British liberal philosophers of the Enlightenment. Their favorite philosopher was the British thinker John Locke. This can be seen in the ideas and phrases lifted from Locke's philosophy to justify the Revolution. Locke stated that government rested upon the consent of the governed and that all men had natural rights upon which no government could legally infringe. Some of these important rights were the right of freedom of thought and belief and property rights. The lower classes, many of whom were illiterate, were not able to access these writings but rather had them passed on to them by the elite members of society who would lead them in the Revolution. In fact, revolutions are not generally lead by the most destitute and illiterate but by the more educated members of society. The poor and downtrodden furnish the foot soldiers for revolution (and incidentally also fill the armies of the anti-revolutionists). In the French and even in the Haitian Revolutions, which were thoroughgoing social revolutions, the leaders were the educated, not the peasants and the slaves. The American Revolution, as we shall see, although radical in its ideology, was a political and not a social, revolution.

It was a short jump from the Enlightenment idea that the world operates in a logical manner to the idea that monarchy is illogical, especially if that monarchy tramples on the natural rights of the people. What could be more irrational—and thus "bad" in Enlightenment thought—than monarchy? Just because a person's father was king and he dies, should the son or daughter become the monarch? This was an insult to the rational thought process of the Enlightenment. Even the deist watchmaker God constructed the world in a logical, rational manner and then stepped back and let it run.

Most of the founding fathers were Freemasons. The Freemasons were important in all four revolutions, with the possible exception of the Haitian revolution, and even there, Masonic concepts of rationality and brotherhood were influential. It is outside the confines of this study to trace the origins of the Freemasons, which have been given racy and questionable origins in such recent works as Dan Brown's *The Da Vinci Code*. Despite their esoteric initiation rites, the Freemasons were primarily a male fraternal organization dedicated to the rational ideals of the Enlightenment. They even parallel Enlightenment religious thinking in that a member is only required to believe in a "higher power" and not a specific organized religion type of God. The lodges of the Freemasons served as revolutionary cells, not only during the American Revolution but in the French and Spanish American Revolutions. Their

George Washington Masonic National Memorial Temple built by Freemasons to honor George Washington.
(Library of Congress)

importance is all the more interesting in predominately Catholic countries, given the church's hostility toward the order. But once again, this highlights the power of Enlightenment ideas, which eschew orthodox religious notions.

The preeminent American Freemason was George Washington. Washington was frequently portrayed dressed in his Masonic apron. The patriots who dressed up as Indians for the Boston Tea Party did so in a tavern, which was a Masonic meeting hall. The Masons were powerful and influential in the American Revolution and thereafter. The very first "third party" (a party outside the two-party system) in American history was the Anti-Masonic Party. They were a group of non-Masons so convinced of the power of the Freemasons, they felt called upon to found an entire political party dedicated to fighting the influence of the Masonic orders. No further proof of the power and influence of the Masons is needed beyond the belief in that power and influence by their contemporaries.

The great pressing need of the British after the French and Indians Wars was for revenue to pay back the huge sums of money that had been necessary to finance the wars. To the English it seemed logical and fair that the Americans pay at least part of the costs of these wars, with the reasoning that they had been fought to protect the Americans from the French and Indian threat. The Americans had fought and died in those wars, and their view was that these sacrifices were sufficient and that the English could not tax them without their consent.

A Belated Attempt to Impose Imperial Control and Taxation

George III, who came to the British throne in 1760, wanted a more hands-on role in governing the American colonies than his predecessors. He also proved to be less astute and less flexible than some earlier kings. He charged his ministers with the task of squeezing revenues out of the colonies and making them obey the Navigation Acts. Thus, he reversed the prior policy of Salutary Neglect, which had ignored American violations of the rules of trade. Since the British had been so inconsistent and lax in the administration of their empire up to this moment and since the Americans has been allowed to run their own affairs to such an extraordinary extent, an explosion on the part of the Americans was inevitable.

George Grenville, Prime Minister from 1763 to 1765, was the instrument of England's new policy toward America. Most importantly, he imposed the Revenue Act of 1764, commonly called the Sugar Act. This act of Parliament imposed stiff taxation on sugar and molasses imported from the French West Indies. Remember that Americans had been flouting trade regulations, like the Molasses Act of 1733, for many years by trading with other than British Caribbean islands. By threatening to vigorously enforce this act, Grenville threatened the New England economy and reversed the policy of salutary neglect.

In response, the colonists asserted that they could only be taxed by their own representatives and they had none in the English Parliament. The English countered that the Americans were "virtually represented" in Parliament, since its members were looking out for American interests. Not surprisingly, Americans did not accept this theory.

Nevertheless, Grenville pushed another tax on the colonies through the Parliament, the Stamp Act. This law required Americans to purchase revenue stamps and affix them to all legal and commercial documents, newspapers, almanacs, playing cards, liquor bottles, and even dice. It was not explained how dice would roll with a revenue stamp attached.

At first a number of Americans signed up to be stamp agents. This was a lucrative post. But the American response to this act was mob violence against the tax collectors and their possessions and houses. Before long, no one was interested in being a stamp tax agent.

The Americans also organized an effective boycott against British manufactured goods. Colonists were persuaded, or intimidated, into not purchasing English goods until the offending legislation was repealed. So effective were these American tactics that Parliament repealed the Stamp Act in 1766. Parliament, however, tried to get in the last word by passing the Declaratory Act. The message was clear: Although the Stamp Act was repealed, England had every right to tax its colonies and would continue to do so. That assertion stoked the sparks of American unrest.

The British would keep trying to tax the colonies. Charles Townsend, Chancellor of the Exchequer (equivalent to the modern U.S. Secretary of the Treasury), in 1767 got Parliament to pass the Townsend Acts. These laws taxed a wide variety of goods in America, such as glass and paint, which had previously not been taxed. The American response was the same as it had been to the Stamp Act—mob violence, backed up by a boycott of British goods. Again the Parliament was forced to relent, repealing all taxes except the tax on tea in 1770.

Many Americans breathed a sigh of relief after the repeal of the Townsend Acts, feeling that the matter of taxation had been settled and that the Parliament was not likely to go down the road of imposed taxation again. Among those hoping for an end to the discord were the wealthiest Americans, those best positioned in society. Even if they agreed with the concept of no taxation without representation, they were repelled by the mob violence that had caused Parliament to back down. After all, such violence could as easily be directed against the upper classes as it could against crown agents. It was only when the English imposed further legislation that threatened the wealthy merchants' livelihoods that some of them swung in favor of independence. They calculated that if a break came with the mother country, the colonial elite could keep the independence movement under their own control. This is precisely the type of thinking that brought the Spanish American Creole elite to the side of independence from Spain and convinced them to keep their revolution in their own hands and to make the break from Spain a political revolution, not a social one. The Spanish American aristocrats had their own nightmare example of mob action, the Haitian Revolution.

▲ The Revolution: A Struggle for Home Rule and Who Will Rule at Home

Even though the majority of Americans were probably satisfied with the repeal of the Townsend Acts, a small group of radical Americans had arisen who opposed even the slightest effort of the British to regulate their colonies. Usually these radicals were what we would call today lower-middle-class individuals. They furnished the leadership for the mob actions that had caused Parliament to back down on taxation.

A leading figure among these middle class radicals was Sam Adams of Boston. He was the second cousin of the more aristocratic John Adams, destined to be the second president of the United States. Sam was a failure as a businessman. He failed as a brewer (though there is a fine beer today named in his honor). He also failed at several other occupations before he found his true calling: professional revolutionary.

Sam Adams and his fellow radicals kept up a steady stream of anti-British propaganda. They exploited such events as the so-called Boston Massacre of 1770. This event had its origins in American feelings of nationalism and economic grievances against British soldiers. As part of their overall policy of trying to run the colonies on the cheap, the English paid their soldiers very little and as a result, the soldiers were forced to look for part-time employment to supplement their pay. This brought them into economic competition with Americans for the same jobs. The events that led up to the massacre began when a mob of Americans, many of whom had just emerged from nearby taverns, began to taunt and jeer British soldiers drawn up on Boston Common. Soon missiles were hurled at the assembled soldiers and they panicked. The soldiers fired into the crowd, killing three Americans, all bachelors. (The significance of the marital status of the dead will be made clear in a moment.)

Adams and fellow radical Paul Revere soon published a series of posters to propagandize the event. As time went on, these posters become more and more fanciful, and soon hundreds of Americans were being mowed down and rivers of blood were flowing. The accompanying narrative to the poster became about the terrible English and how they had deprived so many wives of their husbands and children of their fathers. Remember that the "victims" of the "massacre" were all bachelors. No matter, this was effective propaganda!

The officers of the men who had fired upon the Americans in the Boston Massacre were defended by John Adams, Sam's aristocratic second cousin. This demonstrates that even at this early juncture the principle that all were entitled to a fair trial was well established and boded well for the judicial system after independence. Defending the British was not held against John Adams by the American patriots; otherwise he might never have become the president. The fact that John Adams, an aristocrat, and not Sam Adams, a man of the "middling sort," became a national leader is a demonstration that the American Revolution was to be a political and not a social revolution.

Sam Adams and his fellow radicals also organized "Committees of Correspondence." These committees wrote to each other in an attempt to keep the indignation against the British at fever pitch. Radicals in the colonies compared notes about the latest English outrage in their particular colony.

Sam Adams, "poster boy" of the American Revolution
(Library of Congress)

The Massacre perpetrated in King Street Boston on March 5th 1770, in which Messrs Saml Gray, Saml Maverick, James Caldwell, Crispus Attucks & Patrick Carr were Killed, six others Wounded two of them Mortally

Paul Revere's fanciful poster of the "Boston Massacre"
(Library of Congress)

The final straw that provoked an end to British patience with their colonies was the Tea Act of 1773. The English Parliament and the colonists viewed this act in completely different terms. To the colonists it seemed to be a continuation of the whole series of revenue acts designed to tax the colonies without their consent. The purpose of the Tea Act in English eyes was to bail out the British East India Company. The East India Company had many prominent upper-class investors, and the company was suffering hard economic times. The Tea Act gave the East India Company a monopoly of the tea trade in the colonies. At this time Americans were predominately tea drinkers and not coffee drinkers as they would become later.

The Tea Act and the draconian British efforts to enforce it drove the wealthy merchants toward the cause of independence. They were used to buying their tea wherever they could purchase it most cheaply and the Tea Act threatened their profits. If the English had shown some restraint in the face of American provocations, they might have salvaged the situation. Instead they reacted like the parent of a teenager (which was somewhat how they thought of the colonists) who has finally "had it." After years of disobedience, the British finally snapped. The event that caused this fatal overreaction was the Boston Tea Party. Sam Adams and his compatriots dressed up as Indians (although they weren't fooling anybody) in a tavern in a Masonic meeting hall, proceeded to the docks, and threw the East India Company's tea into the harbor.

The British then responded with what the Americans called the Intolerable Acts. (You can generally tell who the victors are in history by who succeeds in naming events.) These were a strict series of measures to underscore that the English were through indulging the Americans. First of all, Boston Harbor, the city's life blood, was closed until the Americans paid for the tea dumped into the harbor. The American response was the equivalent of "when hell freezes over." The self-governing powers of Massachusetts were curtailed and the Assembly suspended. Eventually the colony would be under virtual military law. English officials would no longer be tried in the colonies for offenses committed there, despite the fact that the officers responsible for the Boston Massacre were given a fair defense. Furthermore, Bostonians were required to board British soldiers in their homes and provide them with beer. This was considered such an outrage that the Third Amendment to the Con-

John Adams
The aristocratic John—and not his middle-class second cousin Sam—became the second president of the United States.
(Library of Congress)

stitution would eventually specifically outlaw the practice of the government quartering soldiers in private homes. Without an understanding of the Intolerable Acts, readers of the Bill of Rights would probably scratch their heads at that amendment.

About the same time the Intolerable Acts were being promulgated, Parliament passed the Quebec Act. This gave to British Canada much of the disputed land that the Americans considered theirs. It also gave religious tolerance to the French Catholic population, a fact that was not appreciated by the predominately Protestant Americans.

These English measures threw the radical propaganda machine into high gear. The cause of Boston was touted as the cause of all the colonies. Other colonies sent food and fuel to the economically blockaded New Englanders.

In this climate of anger, the First Continental Congress met in 1774. All colonies but Georgia sent representatives. The congress met in Philadelphia and because the delegates had been elected in the white-hot anger surrounding the Intolerable Acts, it was a predominately radical body. The congress agreed to what it called the Continental Association. The association decided to try the formerly successful tactic of boycotting English goods. This boycott was to be policed by Committees of Safety. Those who could not be persuaded by patriotic arguments to cooperate with the boycott were often subjected to intimidation, threats, and physical violence. As a result, British imports to the colonies declined.

Die Einwohner von Boston werfen den englisch-oftindischen Thee ins Meer am 18. December 1773.

The Boston Tea Party
Americans, dressed as "Indians," throw tea into Boston Harbor.
(Library of Congress)

There is no way to know whether the majority of Americans agreed with the radicals' tactics. There were no opinion polls. At that point Americans were still not demanding independence but rather a revocation of the Intolerable Acts. Even when independence was subsequently declared, there is no way to determine if that was the will of the majority. Certainly a large number of Americans, called *Loyalists* or *Tories,* continued to support the crown to the point of fighting and suffering for that cause or leaving the country. As in any age, there might have been a large group that was politically indifferent as long as their daily routine was not disrupted. In addition, those on the frontier might not even have heard about the events in Boston.

The spark for war came about when the British determined that they would crush insubordination in Massachusetts. Additional troops were sent to Boston under General Gage. Gage had some sympathy for the Americans. Indeed, his wife was American. Nevertheless, Gage was a good soldier and followed his instructions from the crown. Gage was made military governor.

The Continental Congress had begun to collect arms and train troops, although still not admitting that it was seeking independence. On the morning of April 19, 1775, General Gage sent a group of soldiers outside of Boston to Lexington and Concord, where the Americans were rumored to be collecting arms. Gage also attempted to arrest Sam Adams and John Hancock, but they managed to escape. The colonials were nicknamed "minutemen" because they could be armed quickly. At Lexington the first shots were fired between the Americans and the British, and the revolution was on, although it would be some time before the Americans would admit that they were fighting for independence. The English were highly offended by the military tactics of the Americans, which seemed to have more in common with techniques used by the American Indians as opposed to formal European warfare. The Americans hid behind rocks and trees and harassed the British all the way back to Boston. The English suffered 273 casualties, a huge number of the approximately 700 soldiers who had left Boston.

Political or Social Revolution?

Several simultaneous struggles were going on within the revolution itself. One was to gain support for the independence movement. This issue divided families. For example, while Benjamin Franklin favored independence, his son, the royal governor of New Jersey, was loyal to the crown. Father and son never spoke to each other again.

There was also the question of who would rule in America if the revolution succeeded. The analysis of this issue is most vital to our evaluation of whether the American Revolution was a social or a political revolution. The revolution had opened up leadership possibilities for men of the middle class such as Sam Adams. Leadership by middle class individuals was perhaps the only social aspect of changes resulting from the revolution. There was no question of extending the leadership of the country to lower class white men, who would have to wait until well into the next century under the leadership of Andrew Jackson to come into any kind of power in society. The believers in the natural rights of man did not think of extending political rights to women, even upper class white women. Slaves and Indians were not even to be citizens. Blacks did not become citizens until after the Civil War (even free black men were not citizens under the *Dred Scott* decision of the Supreme Court), and only male African Americans were granted the suffrage after the Civil War. American Indians would not become United States citizens until the late 1880s under the Dawes Act, and then only if they gave up their tribal ways. Women, whose movement for civil rights had begun before the Civil War, debated whether to push for women's suffrage after the Civil War at the same time African American males got the vote. But the majority faction among early feminists decided to step aside in deference to black male voting; it was, they reasoned, "the negroes' hour."

Gordon Wood, one of the greatest historians of the American colonial and revolutionary periods, has to push his analysis in his book *The Radicalism of the American Revolution* (1991) into the 1840s to make any kind of case for the American Revolution being a social revolution. The American Revolution *was* radical in its acceptance of the concept that people could govern themselves without a king or dictator and that a large country, and not just a city state (as in Athens), could function as a democratic republic.

But these changes do not make the American Revolution a social revolution, as the social pyramid did not invert. The king of England was replaced in power by the American aristocrats—slave-holding plantation owners such as George Washington and Thomas Jefferson, and aristocrats of talent, education, and outlook, such as John Adams. In fact, looking at the only other model of democracy in history, the Athenian model, America's aristocrats were far more concerned with the question of whether a republican system could function in a large territory than whether democracy could function concurrently with slavery. The founding fathers even found some reassurance in the fact that a large part of the Athenian population were slaves. Despite Thomas Jefferson's thought of including the abolition of slavery in a draft of The Declaration of Independence, abolition was not the path the Americans chose to take. The northern colonies, in which slavery was not so economically important, were willing to allow its continuation to secure the support of the South. Americans had no chance to defeat the British unless all colonies were on board.

On a philosophical level, Americans were aware of the inherent contradictions between slavery and democracy. As practical men, they needed the support of the colonies where slavery was strongest. Indeed many of the main American aristocrats who would run the government after the Revolution were slave owners, and they were not about making a social revolution. Hypocrisy, however, seldom goes unchallenged in any age. As Samuel Johnson, famous English essayist commented, "Why do the loudest yelps for freedom come from the drivers of Negroes?"

Behind the Victory

Some of my students, invariably male, lament that I do not spend a great deal of time in class on military history, and I do not intend to do so here. I just want to make the following quick points about the Revolution. First, the Revolution took a long time to achieve victory—from 1775, depending on when you wish to date its beginnings, until the peace treaty of 1783, or eight years by this reckoning. Many students assume the Declaration of Independence was published, a few battles were fought, and independence was achieved. That is far from reality. Second, the Revolution was partly a standard war of set-piece battles and partly a guerrilla war. The only famous relative I have from that time period that I know of is Frances Marion, known as "The Swamp Fox." He would hide in the southern swamps, initiate sneak attacks on the English, and fade back into the swamps, which he knew well.

Washington was not a military genius, but he did understand that he could not fight the English army head on. He therefore picked his battles carefully and depended on small victories achieved by stealth, like the battles of Trenton and

Princeton. Also, Washington's commanding presence kept the American army together, even when in retreat.

Historians often take polls to rate our greatest presidents. The three presidents who are always voted into the "great" category are Lincoln, Washington, and Franklin Roosevelt. I agree with the "big three" selections, but not in their order. This book does not deal in detail with Washington's presidency, but I beg your indulgence to make my case for Washington as our greatest president. Lincoln kept the Union together. Franklin Roosevelt saved the capitalist system in America by bending it but not breaking it.

Washington is, I believe, by far our greatest president. Let me count the ways. He truly was the "Father of His Country" by winning the Revolution. He did this at great personal cost. His stature kept the Continental Army together. He devised an effective strategy for winning the war. After the war was over, he went home, although some urged him to put a crown on his head or become a dictator. His country called him back to service at the Constitutional Convention. He was the only choice as our first president. He put the two smartest men in the country into his cabinet, Hamilton and Jefferson. Although I'm sure Washington sometimes longed to crack their squabbling heads together, he suffered through their arguments to receive the best advice. When his two terms were up, Washington went home. That may not sound like a great feat, but consider how many modern heads of state refuse to leave, even if they lose elections. For all these reasons, Washington is, by far, our greatest president.

The other factor that lead to the American victory was help from abroad. The French recognized that the Americans might have a chance to win after their victory at the Battle of Saratoga. The French were willing to send a great deal of money to help the Americans, along with soldiers like Lafayette and the French fleet, which bottled up the English at Yorktown. The French were not compelled by a love of democracy to aid the Americans; their system was a strong monarchy, and their aim was to get back at their old rivals, the British. The American ambassador to France was Benjamin Franklin, who made himself the toast of France by masquerading as a frontiersman, when in fact he had mostly lived in cities. Franklin's ability to flatter the ladies of the French court, who then influenced their husbands toward the American cause, should not be underestimated. The Spanish and the Dutch also contributed money toward the American cause. But it was the French commitment of money, men, and ships that was most instrumental in the American victory. The French monetary contribution to the American victory also helped lead to indebtedness, which helped bring about the fall of the French monarchy, as we shall see in our next chapter.

Benjamin Franklin, ersatz frontiersman and ambassador to France extraordinaire.
(Library of Congress)

When Lord Cornwallis was surrounded by the American and French troops on land on the Yorktown peninsula in Virginia, the British were also hemmed in by sea by the French fleet. Cornwallis and the British army had to surrender, marking the effective end of the war. Surrenders were formal affairs in those days with the commanding officer offering his sword to the victor and the defeated army marching between rows of the victorious troops to lay down their arms. The tune played by the American band that day was most appropriate, "The World Turned Upside Down," for very few in that era felt the Americans could win independence.

One reason for the American victory in the Revolution is the guerrilla war aspects of the struggle. The British were able to land an army wherever they pleased: Long Island, Philadelphia, and Charles Town (it was not to become Charlestown until after the war). They could capture these cities, but they could never pacify the countryside. A guerrilla force can defeat an imperial power by keeping an army in the field, inflicting enough casualties, and costing enough money that the imperial power finally decides the struggle is not worth the mounting price. That is exactly the calculation the English made: They could have continued the fight but it didn't seem worth it. Almost two centuries later, the United States left Viet Nam after ten years and the same calculation. It remains to be seen at this writing how long the United States will stay in Iraq and Afghanistan.

The first system of government under which the United States was governed was the Articles of Confederation, not the Constitution. The Articles dictated a very weak form of national government. The central government had only the powers to conduct foreign affairs, control Indian affairs, set standards of coinage weights and measures, settle disputes among the states, and conduct a postal service. The Confederation could not pass laws directly affecting citizens; only the states could do that. Most importantly, the Confederation lacked the power to tax. It could only get money from the states by asking for "requisitions"—in effect, begging the states for money. Any important law could only be passed with the support of nine of the thirteen states, and the Articles could only be amended with the support of all thirteen states.

One issue and one event finally did in the Confederation. The issue was taxation. Backers of a stronger government proposed an amendment to the Articles to adopt the Impost of 1781, which would raise money for the central government through taxes on imports. But little Rhode Island refused to support the Impost, and the idea died.

The event that helped bring about the demise of the Articles was Shays' Rebellion. Throughout the 1780s, advocates of strong central government fretted about the weaknesses of this form of government. They feared that such a weak government could not even keep order in the new country. Shays' Rebellion confirmed their worst fears.

The rebellion occurred in Massachusetts in 1786 and 1787. Landowners in the state at that time were required to pay their property taxes in specie (gold or silver). Due to economic conditions, many farmers could not pay their taxes, and their farms either had to be sold or foreclosed. Daniel Shays, a veteran of the Revolution, lead the farmers in protest. Sometimes they prevented sheriffs from carrying out foreclosures; sometimes they attacked courthouses to destroy the tax records held within. "Respectable" citizens could only look on impotently as mobs ravished the interior of the state. Because the American army had largely been demobilized after the Revolution, it fell to the wealthy in Boston to finance a militia, which finally put the rebellion down. Those such as George Washington, painfully aware of the weakness of the government of the country he helped to create, began to argue for a stronger central government. Not all the founding fathers were disturbed by Shays' Rebellion. Thomas Jefferson had this to say in a letter to a New York senator:

A little rebellion now and then is a good thing. . . . God forbid we should ever be twenty years without such a rebellion. The people cannot be all, and always, well informed. The part which is wrong will be discontented, in proportion to the importance of the facts they misconceive. If they remain quiet under such misconceptions, it is lethargy, the forerunner of death to the public liberty . . . and what country can preserve its liberties, if its rulers are not warned, from time to time, that this people preserve the spirit of resistance? Let them take arms. The remedy is to set them right as to the facts, pardon and pacify them. What signify a few lives lost in a century or two? The tree of liberty must be refreshed, from time to time, with the blood of patriots and tyrants. It is its natural manure.

The Works of Thomas Jefferson, Vol 5, 1904,
Letter from Jefferson to William Stevens Smith, Nov. 13, 1787

Nevertheless, the advocates of a stronger central government eventually won out. A constitutional convention was called. Its ostensible purpose was to amend the Articles of Confederation. In fact the Congress of the Articles gave its permission for the convention. But the leaders of the convention such as James Madison had no intention of merely amending the Articles, preferring instead a whole new governmental structure, which became the Constitution.

Since the authors of the Constitution had every intention of exceeding their instructions, the convention was held in secret, and no complete record of the debates was kept. Those who want the Constitution interpreted in terms of "original intent," such as current Supreme Court Justice Antonin Scalia, have a problem explaining how they can know what the original intent of the document was, since we have no complete record of the debates upon which it was decided.

Not all patriots agreed that the Articles should be scrapped. Many like, Patrick Henry, argued that the Revolution had been fought precisely to abolish central power, and they were perfectly content with a weak central government. They felt that the state governments, which were supreme under the Articles, were closer to the people and thus more "democratic." Patrick Henry's comment about the Constitutional Convention was, in fact, "I smell a rat!"

▲ The Adoption of the Constitution as a Confirmation of the Political Revolution

The abandonment of the Articles and the adoption of the Constitution can be seen as the final confirmation that the American Revolution was to be a political and not a social revolution. One does not have to completely accept the theories of the historian Charles A. Beard in *An Economic Interpretation of the Constitution* to note that the authors were wealthy educated elites, not small farmers. Beard's main argument is that the Constitution was written by men who were holders of government bonds and who sought a stronger government to make sure that their bonds were paid off.

Consider the undemocratic features of the Constitution. The only officials of the government directly elected were in the House of Representatives. U.S. Senators were elected by the state legislatures until the early twentieth century. To this day, the president is not elected directly by the people but by electors of the inaptly named *Electoral College*. The Electoral College vetoed the will of a plurality of voters in the presidential elections of 1824, 1876, 1888, and most recently 2000. The American aristocrats who designed the Constitution did not believe that the average voter was sufficiently educated to make a direct choice for president. The debate over whether this system disenfranchises voters continues today.

The Pyramid Updated: From King to American Aristocrats

A Political Revolution: John Adams, Not Sam Adams

The American Revolution was a political revolution. It replaced the King of England with American aristocrats (Washington, Jefferson, and John Adams). The social pyramid did not invert. Had the American Revolution been even a minor social revolution, I would argue that Sam Adams and not John Adams might have been our second president. The American aristocrats kept the revolution very much under control and did not allow the lower class, slaves, or Indians to immediately rise in society. As we shall see, this is exactly and self-consciously the type of revolution that the Spanish American Creoles made in their independence from Spain. Yet the American Revolution greatly influenced the next Great Revolution, the French Revolution, which would become the social revolution *par excellence*. The French Revolution would lead, in turn, to the nightmare of all aristocrats, the slave rebellion in Haiti.

The Social Pyramid after the American Revolution

Name: _____ Date: _____

Class: _____

Questions for Reflection and Review

1. Explain the differences between the English colonies and the Spanish colonies. How did these differences affect the differing development of the respective colonial systems? What were the biggest differences between the English and Spanish colonies, and what were the similarities?

_____

_____

_____

_____

_____

_____

2. How consistent were the English in enforcing their regulations in the colonies? How did Americans seek to evade these regulations? In your opinion, did the colonists spend more time "on their own," or under close supervision of the mother country? What skills did the colonists acquire that would aid them as an independent country?

_____

_____

_____

_____

_____

_____

3. At the end of the French and Indians Wars in 1763, the Americans thought of themselves as Englishmen and were proud of their association with the English empire. Yet, in only about a dozen years the Americans were fighting a revolution for independence. What caused this radical change of opinion among Americans?

_____

_____

_____

_____

_____

4. Give your own definitions of a social revolution and a political revolution. In your opinion was the American Revolution predominately political or social, and why?

_____

_____

_____

_____

_____

_____

2 The French Revolution

The Template for All Social Revolutions

The Social Pyramid before the French Revolution

King
of
France

The First
Estate: The
Church 1% of the
population
The Second Estate:
The Nobles 2% of the
population

**The Third Estate: 97%
of the population:**
Lower/ Middle Classes
(Robespierre, Danton)

Peasants

▲ The Example of the American Revolution

The French Revolution is the template by which all social revolutions are judged. When Louis XVI, the King of France, called the Estates General in 1789, nobody could have predicted how far reaching and thoroughgoing a social revolution would result. The American Revolution was a catalyst for the French Revolution in several ways. Most importantly, financing the American Revolution was part of a labyrinth of debt created by the French monarchy that lead to the downfall of the old order. In addition, the American Revolution inspired thoughts of self-government without the need for a king. Although the revolutionaries started with no intention of abolishing the monarchy, as events unfolded and the revolution spun out of control, the elimination of the king became suddenly plausible. French first-hand observers of the American Revolution such as Lafayette glimpsed the possibilities of creating a whole new secular order.

The French aristocrats (nobles) quickly lost control over events and were not able to keep the revolutionary impulse confined to the political realm, as the American aristocrats had been able to do. The king and many of the nobles literally lost their heads, and control of the country passed to the middle and lower classes. The social pyramid inverted and a true social revolution was born. Although the revolution would eventually be overcome by a coalition of conservative European states, the powers and privileges of the king, nobles, and the Church were abolished, never to return in their prerevolutionary form.

The French revolution naturally had a profound effect on French colonies, most notably St. Dominique, or Haiti. Only the most radical of Frenchmen envisioned extending independence to French colonies and the full rights of man to colonials. However, once the revolutionary genie was out of the bottle, it could not be stopped from influencing French territories, ultimately unleashing the only successful rebellion of a slave colony against a European power in the history of the world. The bloody Haitian Revolution in turn presented the Spanish American Creoles with a choice of two different models in their rebellion for independence from Spain. The Creoles of Spanish America who ultimately achieved independence from Spain consciously chose the North American model of political revolution. They did not choose the French-Haitian model of social revolution, which had demonstrated how fatal it was for an aristocracy.

Since the death of Louis XIV in 1715, the quality of the French monarchical administration had declined. Louis XV was a young boy when his father died. A group of nobles had administered Regency during his youth. These nobles had used the opportunity to weaken royal control, and bribery and corruption increased in

France. Middle class bureaucrats, picked for their competency, were passed over in favor of nobles. Financial problems became acute for France, which had fought a series of unsuccessful wars against Great Britain overseas and against Austria and then Prussia on the continent. Taxes were greatly increased to pay for these wars.

Misguided Taxation—Let Them Eat Cake: Taking from the Peasants, Exempting Nobles and the Church

The French tax system was a complicated mass of feudal levies, special taxes on commodities, such as salt, and exemptions that benefited mainly the nobles and the Church. The peasants and middle class were paying much more than their fair share, while the Church and nobles were paying too little. The Church, the greatest landholder in France, and the nobles were protected by ancient "exemptions" dating back to concessions made by kings in the Middle Ages.

When he came into his majority, Louis XV ordered his finance minister, a commoner, to raise taxes via a token land tax on the nobility. The nobles raised such a storm of protest about this that the king backed down and repealed the new levy. During the Seven Years War (called the French and Indian Wars in United States history), Louis imposed a special war tax, one of several that would ultimately be imposed. When French kings couldn't impose further taxation, they often resorted to loans from the large banking houses of Europe, most notably the Rothschilds, to finance wars. Interest repayment would become a larger and larger portion of the French budget, as the country's economic situation declined.

The Weakness of Louis XVI

Louis XV was succeeded by his weak and indecisive grandson, Louis XVI, in 1774. The indecisive nature of the new king contributed mightily to the downfall of the old order in France. Louis's queen was another source of discontent among his subjects. He had married Marie Antoinette of Austria, one of France's old enemies. Although France allied with Austria during the reign of Louis XVI, the old suspicions survived. Many of the common people thought that Marie Antoinette was a spy for her country against France.

Despite the country's heavy debt load, the French decided to finance the Americans in their war of independence against England. This was a chance to get back at France's old enemy England, and perhaps gain back some territory lost in the French

Louis XVI
(Library of Congress)

Marie Antoinette
(Library of Congress)

and Indian Wars. Although the French had the satisfaction of aiding a British defeat, they gained nothing else but additional debt. Eventually, more than 60 percent of France's income was going to meet interest payments.

▲ The Prerevolutionary French Social Pyramid

The American Revolution had arisen out of the most liberal monarchical regime in Europe. The British king was limited by the power of the English parliament. In France, the king was much more powerful. Although France had institutions known as parliaments, they were more judicial than legislative in nature and localized in their jurisdiction. The most they could do was to refuse to publish a law of the king in their jurisdictions; even then the king could override this action by issuing a writ. There were some regional parliaments that acted as quasi-legislative bodies, but there was no equivalent to the national stature and power of the English Parliament.

The closest institution to the English Parliament in France was the Estates General. Kings of France purposely avoided calling the Estates General into session precisely because they wanted to avoid increasing the power of that body. They feared that it might eventually limit the power of the king, as the Parliament did in England. Louis XVI twisted this way and that to try to resolve his financial prob-

A French Enlightenment Trio

Voltaire
(Library of Congress)

Montesquieu
(Library of Congress)

Rousseau
(Library of Congress)

lems. He appointed and fired finance ministers, passed and then repealed revisions of the tax system, and appointed councils of prominent nobles to advise him. None of these expedients brought him any relief for the kingdom's finances. The last recourse was to call the Estates General into session to approve the crucial financial reforms necessary to avoid the regime's collapse.

When the Estates General was finally called in 1789, it was the first time it had met since 1614. The calling of the Estates General, along with the climate of ideas known as the Enlightenment, was a combustible combination set off by the indecisiveness of Louis XVI.

Enlightenment ideas did not cause the French Revolution, but as events evolved, they provided the rationale for increasingly radical changes in the French body politic. Enlightenment thinkers such as Baron Montesquieu, Voltaire, and Rousseau did not even agree on what type of political system France should have. Montesquieu was most interested in a balance of governmental powers that would prevent tyranny by any one branch of government. He would have been willing to retain the king as one branch of the government. Voltaire called for an "enlightened despotism," although he never fully explained what such a system might look like in the real world. He envisioned enlightened rulers applying reforms from above. Voltaire was also hostile to the power of the Catholic Church. Rousseau was the most egalitarian of these thinkers. He felt that mankind had been corrupted by society and that a "social contract" must be worked out whereby no one would envy or have the power to oppress others and society would be governed by the "general will."

Despite the heterogeneity of these ideas, one idea that these *philosophes*, as they were called, all believed was in using human reason to reach solutions for mankind.

They also tended to oppose censorship. Like their American cousins, many men of the Enlightenment in France tended to believe in an abstract deist God, and many were Freemasons. Antipathy toward the Church in France, fanned by the writings of Voltaire and others, were a major factor in alienating the Pope, the upper Catholic hierarchy, and conservative pious peasants from the Revolution.

According to tradition, the Estates General was comprised of three estates, or orders of society. The First Estate was the Clergy, comprising around 1 percent of the population. The Second Estate was the nobles, no more than 2 percent of the population. The Third Estate comprised more than 97 percent of the population, ranging from wealthy tradesmen to starving peasants. Traditionally, each estate had one vote. The first two estates voting together could annul the will of the vast majority of the population.

The main complaints of the people of the Third Estate were the legal and social inequalities in the country and their relative lack of political representation. They also had special grievances about taxation; many of the levies they had to pay had originated in the Middle Ages and lacked any contemporary rational basis. Also, the Third Estate was less able to avoid taxation because they lacked the special privileges enjoyed by the first two estates.

Not surprisingly, the first demands of the Third Estate when called into session with the Estates General had to do with increasing the representation of the huge numbers of citizens they represented. Each estate was supposed to be represented by 300 men each, but the Third Estate selected 600 representatives. They then demanded that the voting system be changed to one man one vote. Such a change would give them an equal number of votes with the first two estates combined.

Louis XVI was called upon to decide the question of one man one vote. He hesitated and was indecisive, as was his nature, but eventually came down on the side of the Third Estate. Although it was not clear at the time, this was probably the king's fatal mistake. Some liberal members of the first two estates then began to vote with the Third Estate, and from that moment on, the Third Estate was in control of events.

The King's Finance Minister, Necker, made a long presentation to the Estates General about the state of the country's finances, but typical of Louis XVI, no concrete proposals were put forward. It was as if, after trying many different approaches to France's financial problems, the king threw up his hands and was asking the Estates General to come up with the solutions.

Since the king seemed willing to cede so much power to the Estates General, they began to see themselves as a legislature, like the English Parliament. The example of the United States and Great Britain of limited monarchy and constitutional rule soon became the ideal of the delegates to the Estates General. They declared themselves to be a National Constituent Assembly that would write a constitution to limit the powers of the king, and they refused to disperse until they had given the country a constitution.

If the Estates General managed to make this change to the National Constituent Assembly permanent, this was indeed revolutionary and the old order of absolutist monarchy would be swept away forever. The opposition to this change by much of the clergy and the nobility made a struggle inevitable. Still there were enough renegade liberal members of the nobility and the clergy in the Constituent Assembly to vote in a constitution.

Louis hesitated. On one hand he did not wish to give up his royal prerogatives. On the other, he was frightened by mobs that had surrounded his palace at Versailles, demanding help with a food shortage and the adoption of a constitution. It is at this point that Marie Antoinette's apocryphal remark "Let them eat cake" was supposedly uttered. Undoubtedly, she never said such a thing, but her ignorance of how the common people lived could well have led her to think it.

The king decided to address the Assembly, but preparations for the meeting were handled by Louis's agents in a clumsy manner. They locked the doors to the meeting hall to make preparations and when the representatives of the Third Estate arrived and found the doors locked, they were angry, thinking they had been excluded. They adjourned to a nearby indoor tennis court and swore the so-called Tennis Court Oath, vowing not to disband until France had been given a constitution. The king then accepted the principle that taxation could not be raised without the consent of the representatives of the nation.

Turning Point: Storming the Bastille

The great symbolic moment of the French Revolution was about to occur. On July 14, 1789, the Parisian mob stormed the Bastille. The Bastille was a royal prison and a symbol of the king's power, as he could traditionally consign someone to the Bastille simply on his own prerogative. The mob that had earlier attacked granaries and bakeries looking for food to ease their hunger now sought arms stored in the Bastille. Much has been made of the release of prisoners held in the Bastille, but fewer than ten prisoners were incarcerated there, as the Bastille had been slated for demolition soon. The main objective of the mob was the arms stored there and the symbolic nature of the prison as a symbol of the king's power to incarcerate based solely on his own ability to issue a writ.

PRISE DE LA BASTILLE

Par les Citoyens de Paris ayant à leurs têtes Mrs les Gardes Françaises, le 14 Juillet 1789

The storming of the Bastille July 14, 1789, was an important symbolic moment of the French Revolution
(Library of Congress)

The governor of the Bastille at first tried to negotiate with the mob and later defended the Bastille less than vigorously. In the mob were some militia and regular army troops who had brought two cannons and knew how to use them. Eventually the Bastille was surrendered. The governor tried to negotiate, but he was eventually killed and decapitated by the mob, which paraded his head on a pike around the city. The fall of the Bastille is seen as a turning point of the Revolution because it marks the emergence of the Parisian mob as a center of political power. Various leaders of the Revolution would compete for the allegiance of the mob, or "the people," as they preferred to call them. The emergence of the lower classes in power also helped sharpen the differences between the French Provinces and the capital, as there was no similar power center in the provinces equivalent to the Parisian mob.

On August 4, 1789, liberal nobles who were cooperating with the Constituent Assembly voted with the majority to renounce their feudal rights. This effectively ended feudalism and the noble's ancient privileges forever. The abolition of peasant duties and payments was also declared; the intention was that some duties would be phased out over time, but peasants, who comprised more than 80 percent of the

French population in the provinces, began to refuse to pay them immediately. They were no longer medieval peasants. A true social revolution had begun.

The militia in Paris was restyled the National Guard and placed under that veteran of the American Revolution, Lafayette. Lafayette would later be seen as a "moderate" in the Revolution and come to grief during the more radical stage of the Revolution. On July 11, Lafayette suggested to the Constituent Assembly the addition of a declaration of rights at the beginning of the new constitution. Lafayette admired the bills of rights included in American state constitutions. The result was the Declaration of the Rights of Man and the Citizen. (French feminists soon created a parallel document for their gender, but it was little noted at the time.)

Lafayette
Veteran of the American and French Revolutions
(Library of Congress)

In typical Enlightenment style, the document proclaimed the natural rights of men to include "liberty, property, security and resistance to oppression." It provided for a separation of powers in the government, reflecting the ideas of Montesquieu. Law was declared the expression of the "general will," a nod to Rousseau. Men were born free and were equal in rights. Criminal defendants were innocent until proven guilty, and there was to be freedom of speech and opinion. Taxation, the great spark for the Revolution, would be "equal." And all men were to participate personally or through their representatives in government. There were no personal attacks on the king as there had been in America under the Declaration of Independence, because the king was intended, at this point, to be part of the governmental system. By late 1789, the king and queen were virtual prisoners of the Parisian mob and the Assembly was forced to move from Versailles to Paris.

The Role of the Church ②

The question of the role of the Catholic Church was one of the sticking points in the Declaration. Members of the assembly agreed on a compromise that no one would be molested for his religious beliefs as long as he observed the civil peace. This compromise was not anti-religious or anti-Catholic. It granted more religious freedom

Anti-clerical cartoon reflecting the French revolutionaries' contempt for the Church and the Pope
(Library of Congress)

than had ever existed in France. In view of the anti-clericalism of many of the authors of the declaration, it is probably the best the Catholic Church could have hoped for at that point in the Revolution.

It is important to differentiate between anti-clericalism and anti-Catholicism. Anti-clericalism basically reflects hostility to the political and economic power of the Church and not to its theology. It would allow the Church to minister in the spiritual realm but sought to remove its power in otherwise secular realms such as land ownership and education. Anti-clericalism would be a potent force in both the French and Spanish American Revolutions. The United States, because of its multiplicity of religious beliefs, would rely on separation of church and state. Since France and Spanish America were almost totally Catholic, different arrangements would arise. In Haiti, various African religions and Voodoo competed with the Catholic Church, causing the Haitian Revolution to be different yet in its approach to the religious question.

The law that brought the struggle between the Revolution and the Catholic Church to a head was the Civil Constitution of the Clergy passed by the Assembly in 1790. This proved to be perhaps the biggest mistake by the Assembly. It caused unnecessary conflict between strict Catholics, many of whom were in favor of other revolutionary ideas, and anti-clericals. A more moderate approach to Church reform legislation might have given the anti-clericals more time and energy to spend on other revolutionary goals. But French anti-clericals could not help themselves; they were acting in the same manner as eighteenth and nineteenth century Enlightenment anti-clericals elsewhere, such as in Spanish America (as we will see in Chapter 4). The difference between the religious issue in the American Revolution and its role in the French, Haitian, and Spanish American revolutions is that religious pluralism in the United States caused the struggle to be directed against the establishment of any one church as the official church. Enlightenment impulses in Catholic countries could only express themselves in the form of anti-clericalism. Many peasants who otherwise supported the radical goals of the revolution, such as dismantling feudalism, would rebel against the revolutionary government when they believed their beloved Church was threatened.

The Civil Constitution of the Clergy allowed the state to confiscate church property and made priests employees of France. Later monks and nuns would be turned out of their monasteries. Living a life sequestered from society did not square with Enlightenment concepts of all citizens as independent beings, with no special rights and immunities, fully involved in life and all engaged in a fair competition on a level playing field.

French priests were now employees of France. If they wanted to be paid, they needed to take an oath required by the revolutionary state. This put priests in a difficult position, all the more so because it took the papacy more than a year to decide whether priests should comply and take the oath. Finally, in April 1791, Pope Pius VI ordered priests not to take the oath and those who had taken the oath to renounce it on pain of excommunication. Priests and laypeople were split over whether priests should swear allegiance to the new government. Realizing the counterproductive nature of this controversy, the Assembly attempted to alleviate it with legislation passed in May 1791. This legislation allowed priests who had not sworn the oath to rent church property to say masses. This legislation exacerbated rather than calmed the storm, as some Catholics stood by the "revolutionary" priests, while others backed those who had not taken the oath. Anti-clericalism was a thicket that revolutionaries entered at great risk and that put the revolution in danger from within.

A New Constitution—and the End of the Monarchy

By 1791, the new Constitution had been completed. It called for powers to be shared between the king and Parliament, along English lines. The king endorsed the constitution. The power of the French Parliament was to be ever greater than that of the English Parliament. Earlier the Assembly had taken up the issue of who would vote. There was never a possibility that women would be enfranchised. The struggle was over whether all male Frenchmen would be able to vote. The Assembly made a curious distinction between "active citizens" and "passive citizens." Active citizens were those who owned a certain amount of property and could vote. Passive citizens were those who had natural and civil rights but could not vote. This distinction paralleled the voting system in the United States at the time. It was so unpopular in France that it was eliminated before the constitution was adopted. Nevertheless it demonstrates how in the early stages of the revolution, only propertied men were considered worthy of exercising the franchise. The initial retention of the king and the concept of propertied male voters are indications that not all conservative ideas had yet been swept away by the French Revolution.

Indecision on the part of Louis XVI continued to undermine his status in France. While he resented the curtailment of his prerogatives, the king continued to passively go along with the measures of the government, endorsing them whenever he was called upon to do so. Louis XVI alternated between passive resistance to the Revolution and the notion of perhaps fleeing the country and allying with the reactionary kings of Europe in the hope they might somehow support him and reinstall him as an absolute king. His desire to escape "house arrest" led to a bizarre incident known as the "Flight to Varennes."

Georges Jacques Danton
Middle-class French revolutionary leader
and rival to Robespierre
(Library of Congress)

In April 1791, the king had wanted to go to one of his family houses in the countryside but was prevented by the Paris mob. One of the reasons the king wanted to leave the capital was to take the sacraments from a priest who had not sworn the revolutionary oath. A more serious attempt to escape occurred in the middle of the night of June 20, 1791. This was an attempt to reach the border of France where Louis XVI might get reinforcements from other European countries that might then return the king to the throne with his former power restored. At Varennes, troops loyal to the king were to rendezvous with the royal family, but they did not materialize. Instead, troops loyal to the revolution captured the royal family and transported them back to Paris. The king and queen's attempt to escape Paris made his acceptance of the new constitution appear to be a sham, if his secret plan was to escape and raise an army to overthrow the revolution. More radical revolutionaries had always suspected the king's loyalty. Now the king and queen were universally suspected of trying to undo the revolution. This suspicion ultimately led to their deaths. The attempted flight of the king also strengthened the position of those who wanted a republic, doing away with the monarchy altogether. Here again, the American Revolution was the inspiration.

Also in 1791, a national election was called to select the new National Assembly, as the Parliament was called. It was in this atmosphere of change that political "factions," or parties, were formed. Two middle class leaders who would lead a genuine social revolution rose through the ranks of these political parties, or "clubs." Paris was divided into political districts for electoral purposes and in one of these, the Cordeliers District, a political party or club arose called the Cordeliers Club. It advocated municipal government by direct democracy. The outstanding political leader who arose from the Cordeliers Club was Georges Jacques Danton. Danton was originally a lawyer from provinces with an imposing physique and a powerful speaking style. He was thirty at this point of the revolution.

MORT DE LOUIS XVI, LE 21 JANVIER 1793

Place de la Concorde : on voit à gauche le socle de la statue de Louis XV déboulonnée

(Extrait des *Révolutions de Paris*)

The Execution of Louis XVI
(Library of Congress)

Maximilien Robespierre
Both he and Danton would eventually fall from power during the Terror.
(Library of Congress)

The other outstanding middle class revolutionary destined to lead the social revolution was Maximilien Robespierre. Robespierre was associated with the Jacobin Club, one of the most radical of the political factions. The Jacobins gained their name from their meeting place, a former monastery. More moderate revolutionaries such as Lafayette formed the Society of 1789. The fact that the more radical members of the French legislature tended to sit on the left side of the assembly hall and the more conservative members sat on the right side, led to our use of the terms *left* and *right* to designate liberal and conservative political views today.

Since the beginning of the French Revolution, the revolutionaries had been afraid of foreign intervention to attempt to overthrow the revolution. The conservative kingdoms of Europe, aware of the "bad" example of limitation of kingly power, would indeed have liked to overturn the revolution. However, the mutual suspicions of each other's territorial motives limited their cooperation against the French revolutionaries. The attempted flight of Louis XVI reinforced those who saw enemies of the revolution in reactionary Europe. In 1792 France declared war on Prussia and Austria. For the rest of the revolution, France would be at war not only internally but externally. Of the four revolutions explored in this text, only the French occurred in the "mother" country. The other three revolutions (American, Haitian, and Spanish American) were a matter of colonies attempting to throw off the mother country.

The attempt of the king to flee the country and the declaration of war on Austria and Prussia changed the atmosphere within France. Until 1792, the moderates, who wanted to maintain the monarchy and who wanted to avoid any challenge to the rights of property, were in control. Now the radical middle class Jacobins took over the Assembly. The moderates were driven into silence or exile. For instance, the Jacobins accused Lafayette of treason and tried to impeach him in the Assembly. Although the resolution of treason was ultimately defeated, Lafayette was eventually declared to be an outlaw by the government and went into exile. The Austrians did not trust Lafayette either, fearing him as a revolutionary, and kept him imprisoned for five years.

The Jacobins were determined to extend the revolution and put the "common man" in charge. They wanted obliterate any remaining aristocratic privilege and end royal power. They tended to see a great number of enemies of the revolution inside of France, and when Prussian and Austrian troops actually crossed the border into France, their fears reached fever pitch. They soon could not distinguish between those who disagreed with them and those who were genuine enemies of the revolution.

On August 6, 1791, large demonstrations in Paris called for the king to abdicate the throne. The Assembly, which had refused to impeach Lafayette, also refused to dethrone the king. On August 10, the radicals attacked city hall and replaced the city government of Paris with a radical body called the Commune. The king fled for safety to the Legislative Assembly, but the Assembly was surrounded by a mob. Under pressure from the mob and the Commune, the Assembly suspended the king from the government. The fate of the king was to be left up to a convention that would be elected to change France from a constitutional monarchy to a republic. The events of August 10, 1791, are often called the "Second French Revolution."

The newly elected Convention was based on the American Constitutional Convention. Unlike the American convention, however, the French body did not write a constitution and then disband, but rather stayed in session to pass legislation and run the country. Before the Assembly passed power over to the Convention, it adopted one crucial piece of legislation: Marriage was declared by law to be a civil contract. The fact that marriage was no longer a religious institution but a civil one underscored further the process of separation of church and state. In the same vein, the registration of births, deaths, and marriages was transferred from the church to the state, and divorce was allowed. Even though the French Revolution did not give women the right to vote, it did declare them equal within the state of marriage.

The French army was able to stop the advance of the Prussians at the Battle of Valmy, and this gave the Convention a little breathing space to continue the revolution. The Convention, like the Assembly before it, was divided into factions (quasi-political parties). The Mountain, so called because its members sat on the left side in the upper seats, depended on the poor of Paris for its support. The Parisian poor were also referred to as *sans-culottes,* since they could not afford the fancy breeches worn by the wealthy. The Girondins took their name from the fact that several of their leaders came from the Gironde area. The unaligned members of the Convention were referred to as "the Plain," or "the Marsh." These new groupings often overlapped with the older factions, such as the Jacobins, creating a rich and complex stew of intermingled interests and political views.

Dr. Joseph-Ignace Guillotine
His invention, the guillotine, was to
become synonymous with the terror of
the French Revolution.
(Library of Congress)

The Girondins were a great deal more concerned with the violence of the Revolution and thus were more "conservative" than the Mountain. The Mountain was closely associated with the Jacobins, and soon those two terms were synonymous. *Jacobin* became the term both inside and outside of France to denote the most radical of the revolutionaries. To foreign conservatives, *Jacobin* became an epithet to describe the worst excesses of the Revolution. The Jacobins accused the Girondins of cooperating with the king.

The Convention was to decide the fate of the king. The Jacobins did not even think the king deserved a trial. Robespierre declared that the king was already convicted in the eyes of the nation. The Girondins, however, wanted to observe legal practices, and a trial of the king for treason was held. The Convention found the king guilty of treason almost unanimously, with 361 members voting for the death penalty without conditions and 360 voting for some kind of a lesser penalty. Louis XVI was executed by guillotine in January 1793, and Marie Antoinette suffered the same fate in October of the same year. The ultimate fear of conservatives, regicide, had now come to pass.

▲ The Pyramid Inverted: The People in Charge

The execution of the king divided public opinion both inside and outside of France. The execution shocked many educated Europeans, even some who had supported the revolution. Opinion in the United States was likewise divided and tended to break down according to faction in U.S. politics. As we shall see, those in the Federalist faction, like Alexander Hamilton, tended to oppose the French Revolution, while those who would come to be called Republicans, led by Thomas Jefferson, tended to support the revolutionaries. What had begun as a campaign for justice in France soon degenerated into a bloodbath.

Louis's method of execution, the guillotine, came to symbolize the next phase of the Revolution. Louis XVI himself had outlawed the practice of execution by "breaking on the wheel" (the gory details of which I will spare the reader), although its use was retained in the French colony of Haiti. <u>The Assembly had set up a committee to arrive at a more humane method of execution.</u> This was seen as a "reform," since the reason for execution was to end life and not to inflict gratuitous pain. The committee, including a professor of anatomy, Dr. Joseph-Ignace Guillotine, came up with a machine with a sharp blade that decapitated with surgical precision. It would claim thousands of victims before the revolutionary fires burned out.

The radicals, especially the Jacobins, became more and more concerned to discover enemies of the revolution both within and outside of France. The international situation was exacerbated when French armies defeated the Austrians to control the former Austrian Netherlands.

The guillotine as a diabolical device
(Library of Congress)

The Convention now declared that France was no longer fighting only to protect itself but also to liberate peoples in all of Europe. The French armies now threatened Holland. England could not allow France to cut off its trade access to the continent, and soon France found itself fighting Holland and England as well.

The French general in charge of the campaign, General Dumouriez, now declared himself a believer in constitutional monarchy and not a republic and defected to the Austrians. Since Dumouriez was associated with the Girondins, the Jacobins used this fact to paint all Girondins as disloyal to the revolution.

Because the French were desperately in need of more troops, a system of regional quotas was established to ensure that each part of the country would provide its fair share of men. The provinces around Paris and in the east tended to fill their quotas, but in some areas of the western part of France, there was widespread opposition to a draft. The more conservative peasants now raised their own army, the Catholic and Royal Army. As the name implies, these people wanted the return of monarchy and the powers of the Church. Although the rebellion was put down, it further accelerated the fear of internal traitors to the Revolution. The French economy, groaning under the expenses of war and internal revolt, suffered a meltdown. By 1793, the value of the currency fell by half.

In view of these crises, the Convention took steps to increase central power. A Committee of General Security was set up to concentrate on matters of treason and internal dissent. The twelve members of this committee were chosen from among the members of the Convention. A Revolutionary Tribunal was established to deal with enemies of the revolution. Local vigilante committees supplemented the work of the Tribunal. The most important innovation of the time was the creation of a Committee on Public Safety. This committee eventually took over from the ineffective Executive Committee of the Convention. The members of the Committee on Public Safety were to be elected every month from among the members of the Convention. At the beginning this committee was dominated by Danton. The conflict between radicals and moderates widened. Eventually the Committee on Public Safety would run France with dictatorial powers, and all who were not considered sufficiently revolutionary would feel its wrath, up to and including the death penalty.

The Rise and Fall of Revolutionary Leaders: Marat, Danton, and Robespierre

Jean-Paul Marat, a middle-class, fire-breathing journalist and medical doctor, came into conflict with the government by opposing the original declaration of war in 1792. He styled himself a friend of the people and a firm believer in the will of the people. He called for a dictator to save the revolution and for the use of any means necessary against supposed enemies of the state. He was elected a member of the Convention, where his rhetoric frightened the more moderate members of that body, including the Girondins.

Marat's enemies decided to deal with him by bringing him up on charges before the Revolutionary Tribunal for attacking the Convention. The Girondins supported the charges against Marat, while the Jacobins opposed them. The Tribunal, intimidated by demonstrations in favor of Marat, acquitted him. The mob now demanded that the Convention be purged of the Girondins who had prosecuted Marat. Eventually all the Girondins were purged from the Convention, placing the radical Jacobins firmly in control.

Marat resigned from the Convention after his acquittal. He was seriously ill with a skin disease that made even wearing clothes painful. He continued his work as a journalist while seated in a bath tub with a board across it to serve as a work space. A young woman named Charlotte Corday went to his house claiming to have information on traitors to the revolution. She was actually there to avenge the expulsion of the Girondins from the Convention. She knifed Marat to death and suffered the death penalty herself, being executed by guillotine. This one incident demonstrates in microcosm the type of internecine warfare that occurred during the bloodiest part of the Revolution, which became known as the Terror. It elevated the status of Marat within the revolutionary movement to that of a martyr.

Events in Paris caused a rebellion among the more conservative people living outside the capital. This is sometimes referred to as the Federalist Revolt because it was partly a reaction against the centralization of power in Paris to the supposed detriment of the rest of France. What is particularly striking about the Federalist Revolt was that it occurred in the three largest cities outside of Paris, Marseilles, Lyon, and Bordeaux, as well as in a province known as the Vendée in western France. Another motivation for this revolt was the purging of the Girondins from the Convention. The Jacobins saw the revolt not as a protest for more regional power but as treason. This revolt was not stamped out by the central authorities until the fall of 1793; along with the external wars France was fighting, it accelerated the paranoia of the Jacobins. This lead to the bloodiest period of the French Revolution, called the Reign of Terror.

Danton fell from power on the Committee of Public Safety by failing to win reelection. This brought Robespierre to power. The expression "the revolution devours its own children" was never truer than in the French Revolution. Both Danton and Robespierre were destined to be executed in the orgy of recrimination and madness that became the Revolution.

The Convention decided that to provide manpower for the Republic's foreign wars, drastic changes would be needed in the way the army was staffed. Therefore, a *levee en masse* was instituted proclaiming that the entire people were responsible for the defense of the nation. Men would be sent to the army as needed, and all citizens were expected to help the war effort in any way they could. This was a stark break from the past in which countries had depended on professional soldiers. It prefigured the concept of total mobilization of the population for war, which would not be seen again on this scale until World War I.

Robespierre became the spokesman for the Committee of Public Safety. He was a bachelor who lived in an austere manner and was completely devoted to the revolution, causing his followers to refer to him as "the incorruptible." Robespierre and the Committee saw enemies everywhere. Anyone judged not sufficiently revolutionary was imprisoned and often executed. It is estimated that between 25,000 and 40,000 victims were guillotined, and many thousands more were exiled or imprisoned by Courts of the People during the Reign of Terror in 1793 and 1794. Eventually even Danton and Robespierre would meet this fate. Finally, the Terror struck so many that it could no longer be tolerated.

The fall of Danton was precipitated by several factors. Unlike Robespierre, Danton enjoyed living well. His income increased during the Revolution, and his enemies accused him of taking bribes. Danton had once been allied with Robespierre but the pair had a falling out. Danton had taken a vacation to his estate and returned to Paris to advocate a moderation of the Terror. For all these reasons and to eliminate him as an alternate center of power, the Committee had him indicted and tried for conspiring against the Revolution. The verdict was a forgone conclusion, but Danton maintained a dark sense of humor. When he learned that he was to be guillotined, Danton is supposed to have remarked, "Above all, don't forget to show my head to the people: It's worth seeing."

Robespierre then decided that to unite France he needed to create a civic religion. In this he was looking back to the days of classical Rome when the official religion was one of state. The artist Jacques-Louis David, a member of the Committee, created the ceremony and the decorations for the launching of the Cult of the Supreme Being. (David also painted many scenes of the Revolution, including the famous depiction of the death of Marat.) On May 7, 1794, the cult was inaugurated with great pomp and fanfare. The Cult of the Supreme Being, however, never caught on with the French people.

A thoroughgoing social revolution, the French Revolution sought to change everything about French society. A whole new calendar was adopted with the beginning of the Revolution as Year One. The system of measurements was changed and the metric system was invented. Anti-clerical legislation sought to control the power of the Catholic Church and harness it to the needs of France. The Cult of the Supreme Being was introduced as an attempt to attach all citizens to the state through a common civic religion. A new educational system, based on the theories of Rousseau, was planned but never implemented. The revolutionaries were attempting to supplant the old order with a totally new society.

By 1794 the French had created an army of 200,000, a huge force for the time. By force of numbers, the French were winning their foreign wars, and the Terror could no longer be justified on the basis of military threat from outside. A natural reaction set in against the bloodshed of the Terror. The people of France were exhausted and yearned for a respite from white-hot revolutionary zeal, paranoia, and, bloodshed. This mood is symbolized by the fall of Robespierre.

Members of the Committee of Public Safety began to feud among themselves. They worried that if a former member of the Committee, Danton, could be executed, they themselves might be next. Robespierre's enemies on the right and left united to dispose of him. He was denounced as a tyrant. The Convention condemned Robespierre to death and the people of Paris, perhaps worn out by the quickly shifting times of the revolution, failed to spring to his aid. Robespierre attempted to commit suicide by jumping from a window, but only managed to paralyze himself. On July 28, 1794, Robespierre was executed, and eighty-three of his supporters soon suffered the same fate. The fall of Robespierre and his colleagues symbolized the end of the Terror and the beginning of a reaction.

Moderates and royalists were then released from prison and began to hunt down and kill the radicals who had persecuted them. There was another rebellion against the central government. The government managed to get some of the insurgents to lay down their arms by promising a more moderate religious policy toward the Church. Women, in particular, led the way in helping the conservative clergy resume regular masses. There was even some suggestion that a monarchy might be reinstated.

A new constitution called for a two-house legislature, did away with universal male suffrage, and omitted the clause calling for equality of citizens from the Bill of Rights. There were tax-paying qualifications for voting, and the age when men could vote was raised to twenty-one. The executive power of France was now vested in five men known as the Directory. A Council of Elders (all at least forty years old) would choose the Directors. One Director would retire each year, and another would be chosen by the Elders. This period of French history is referred to as the Directory and constitutes the beginning of the end of revolutionary ardor.

Echoes of the Revolution in American Politics

The Directory lasted about five years. Until 1798, the foreign wars went well for France. The contest between France and Britain ensnared the Americans. The United States insisted that as a neutral nation (neutrality had been declared by President George Washington), it had a right to trade with both sides. Unfortunately, the new nation did not have the naval power to enforce its trade policies. The British, in particular, had a nasty habit of seizing American ships that traded with the French and forcing American sailors into service in the Royal Navy. Washington sent John Jay to England in an attempt to stop British depredations against American shipping. Jay returned with a treaty that seemed to its foes an almost total capitulation to British terms. During the debate over Jay's Treaty in the Senate, American political factions crystallized into genuine political parties. The Federalists, led by Hamilton, tended toward the English side in the European wars, while the Republicans under Jefferson sided with the French.

The French, angered by Jay's Treaty, then began to seize American ships that traded with England. The United States was caught between the major European sea power, England, and the major land power, France. Owing a large measure of its independence to French help, the United States was also bound by treaty to support

John Adams, second president of the United States
He wisely avoided war with France.
(Library of Congress)

France. The European conflict allowed the United States to secure its borders with Spain and gain the right to ship freely on the Mississippi River, when Spain shifted from the British side to the French side in 1795 and realized the vulnerability of Florida and Louisiana.

As the leader of the Federalists, Hamilton demanded war against France. But the new President, John Adams, also a Federalist, wisely resisted the pressure for war, realizing the utter unpreparedness of his young country. Adams sent a mission to France to try to end the naval war and to revoke the treaty with France, which technically France could have invoked to compel the Americans to fight on its side against the English. The French Directory government was developing a reputation for corruption, which was on display in the so-called "XYZ Affair." Certain French ministers, referred to in American dispatches as Minister Y, Minister X, and Minister Z, demanded bribes to expedite the agreement Adams sought. Adams recalled the American diplomats, and an undeclared naval war began between France and the United States. Adams kept his head and sent another mission to France in 1799, which achieved an end to the war and an end to the Franco-American treaty of alliance.

While Adams deserves credit for not sending the United States unprepared into war, he gave in to Hamiltonian extremists in another way. In 1798, the Alien and Sedition Acts were passed by Congress and signed by President Adams. These are best understood as the growing pains of a democracy. They also reflect the fear and hysteria about the possible spreading of Jacobin ideas in the United States. They represent a curtailment of civil rights, which the United States tends to lapse into in times of danger. Thus, we have Lincoln's suspension of habeas corpus during the Civil War, the Sedition Act during World War I, the internment of Japanese Americans during World War II, and, most recently, the Patriot Act. Fortunately, once a crisis has moderated, cooler heads tend to prevail and civil liberties are reinstated, such as in the recent Supreme Court decisions re-extending habeas corpus rights to prisoners held for years without trial by the Bush administration at Guantanamo Bay in Cuba.

The Alien Act allowed President Adams to deport any alien he thought dangerous. This was particularly aimed at agents of the French Revolution sent to the United States to stir up support for the Revolution. Although no aliens were actually deported by Adams, many left in fear of deportation. The Federalists had also noted that immigrants tended to become members of the Republican Party once they were naturalized. The Alien Act, therefore, extended the residence requirement for U.S. citizenship from five to fourteen years. Most of the same arguments made for and against immigration more than two hundred years ago are the very ones heard today.

The Sedition Act called for fines of up to $5,000, a huge sum at the time, and imprisonment for up to five years for persons who conspired to oppose government measures, who promoted riots or unlawful assemblies, or who published any "false, scandalous and malicious writing against the government or its officials." This was an obvious violation of freedom of speech and the press protected by the First Amendment to the Constitution, but it appealed to the thin-skinned, vain Adams. In Adams's defense, we should point out that democracy was a new experiment, and presidents were not used to the type of lusty criticism we take for granted today.

Nevertheless, eleven Republicans editors were indicted under the Sedition Act, and ten were convicted, including a Congressman, Matthew "the Spitting" Lyon. Lyon had received his nickname by spitting on a rival in Congress. Lyon was reelected to Congress by his constituents from his jail cell. Thus, the French Revolution had important ramifications in the United States.

In France, the Government of the Directory was criticized by both the political right and left. The Directory was supposed to bring about a democracy, but time and time again it manipulated or annulled elections. Some of the Directors also became wealthy through graft.

A conspiracy of the left was discovered by the Directory. A man named Babeuf created a quasi-socialist movement; in later years, Marxists would try to claim this movement as a precursor to communism. The Directory took advantage when putting down Babeuf's movement to also prosecute Jacobins who didn't even know Babeuf.

Royalists now founded their own political movement, the Club de Clichy. This coalition included those who wanted a constitutional monarchy, as well as those who desired an absolute monarch. In the election of 1797, a large number of royalists were elected to the legislature. The Directory, in conjunction with the military, selectively annulled the election results, voiding the election of 177 representatives. It also sent troops to the chambers of assemblies and arrested and deported about fifty-three royalists. The Directory was determined not to let either the Jacobins on the left or the royalists of the right undermine its power. The Directory dropped all pretense of democracy and ruled with the support of the army.

The Directory was anti-clerical, fearing the political power of a resurgent Catholic Church. Nevertheless, after the end of the Terror, a Catholic revival was in full swing. The Directory tried to impose a new Civil Cult based on deistic beliefs with an admixture of ancient Greek practices, Confucius, and the Koran. It appealed to very few and was not much more successful than Robespierre's attempt to instill a civic religion. The Directors also desired to have lay teachers in classrooms and not priests. The Directory instilled these same religious concepts in foreign areas captured by French armies. Territory was taken from the Papal States, and the Pope was treated very harshly. In 1799 French armies captured the Pope, and he died in their custody. Only when Napoleon took power were cordial relations reestablished with the Papacy.

Since the Directory was propped up by the army, generals became national heroes. The plunder of war also provided income for the Directory, so there was no incentive to end conflict. In 1795, Prussia sued for peace. Also, the Dutch and Spanish signed peace treaties. The Directory established Holland as a democracy. Greatly aiding French military success was the fact that Austria, Prussia, and Russia were all at each other's throats. Britain dominated the sea but did not have a large land army. England tried to undermine France by financing the military operations of its continental rivals.

In the military campaign of 1796 General Napoleon Bonaparte came to the fore. He was born to the minor aristocracy of the island of Corsica, which then belonged to France. Napoleon was originally aligned with the Jacobins through Robespierre's brother and witnessed Robespierre's fall. Napoleon was briefly imprisoned as a follower of the Jacobins but quickly released. He gained favor with the Directory by helping them put down an uprising. However, Napoleon soon began to follow his own policy and not that of the Directory.

The British attempted to take advantage of their naval superiority by taking over French colonies in the Caribbean. A slave rebellion broke out in St. Dominique (Haiti) in 1791. (This rebellion will be explored in the next chapter.) The English attempted to take advantage of this unrest by getting the white French planters on their side. The English landed troops in Haiti in 1793 and later captured the French colonies of Guadeloupe and Martinique.

Liberty, Equality, and Fraternity for the Colonies?

In 1792 the French sent emissaries to Haiti to appeal to the small percentage of free black people. The Spanish, who controlled the eastern two thirds of the island of Hispaniola (today's Dominican Republic), tried to establish an alliance with Haiti's rebelling slaves, with an eye toward eventually retaking the whole island. Spain, of course, had originally possessed all of Hispaniola after Columbus's Caribbean voyages.

Sonthonax, the French Convention's envoy to Haiti, was convinced that France would lose the colony if some gesture was not made toward improving the lot of the slaves. The Convention, however, had no intention of extending the rights of man, let alone liberty, quality, and fraternity, to the slave possessions of France. When the French government changed to the Convention, the abolition of slavery was proclaimed, not because of moral conviction but because it seemed the only way to hang on to the island. The Haitians (correctly) suspected this gesture by France and kept on fighting.

The Haitians were right to suspect French motives, as Napoleon soon repealed the grant of freedom to the Haitian slaves, recaptured Guadeloupe and Martinique, and reimposed slavery there.

One of the most remarkable and wrongly ignored figures in world history, Toussaint L'ouverture, emerged as the leader of Haiti. He would not only defeat French troops sent to put down the rebellion (the same troops who had defeated almost every country in Europe) and secure the independence of Haiti, he also outplayed the Spanish and took over the entire island of Hispaniola. Toussaint's remarkable story will be told in Chapter 3.

The French planned to invade England and, to expedite this, stir up rebellion in England's colony, Ireland. Napoleon was named the commanding general of the "Army of England."

Napoleon Bonaparte
He ended the French Revolution, lost Haiti, precipitated the Spanish American Revolution, and created the conditions for the United States to acquire all of the Louisiana Purchase.
(Library of Congress)

Once again, however, Napoleon had a different agenda than the Directory. Instead, Napoleon convinced the Directory to send his army to Egypt. The reasons for Napoleon's expedition are obscure. He sold it as a way of disrupting communications for Britain's empire to the east. Napoleon admired Alexander the Great and may have considered establishing his own empire in the former lands of Alexander.

Napoleon's invasion of Egypt created an alliance of convenience between the Ottoman Empire (whose territory was invaded), its old enemy Russia, and Great Britain against France. Although the campaign originally went well, it soon bogged down. At the same time, France's enemies began to defeat French armies in Europe. Napoleon seized on the defeats in Europe as an excuse to return to France. (He made a habit of this sort of thing, later abandoning his troops in Russia when things were not going well.) The Egyptian campaign ended as a fiasco. The major accomplishment turned out to be the discovery of the Rosetta stone, the key to decoding Egyptian hieroglyphics.

French military losses in 1799 put the Directory under further pressure. The Directors continued to annul and cancel elections as a means to continue in power. The elections of 1798 had seen a resurgence of Jacobinism, but this was negated when the Directory simply replaced elected leftists with its own supporters.

When Napoleon landed back in France, a couple members of the Directory decided to conspire with Napoleon to bring about a coup. Napoleon was supposed to furnish the prestige and military backing for the coup. Instead, Napoleon outmaneuvered the politicians and took power himself. He styled himself the First Consul and made the other conspirators merely advisors.

⚬ A Revolution Ends, Conflict Continues

The coup by Napoleon in November 1799 is generally seen as the end of the French Revolution. He himself declared that the Revolution was completed. However, certain ideas of the Revolution, such as promotion based on merit and not circumstances of birth, continued in France and were extended to other Europeans countries by Napoleon's army. Napoleon was the military genius of the age, and it took a large coalition of countries until 1815 to finally defeat him. However, Napoleon's troops could not defeat a rag-tag band of slaves in Haiti and their brilliant commander, Toussaint L'ouverture.

Napoleon had dreamed of an American empire based on Haiti and Louisiana. Once Haiti was lost, Napoleon astonished emissaries from the United States by not only offering to sell New Orleans but the entire Louisiana Purchase. This purchase doubled the size of the United States.

Napoleon established a Concordat with the Vatican in 1801. This made Catholicism the semi-official religion of France but it also pleased anti-clericals by making the Church and clergy part of the state and putting them under state control. Napoleon reformed the laws of France, administrative and judicial systems were streamlined, and the provinces were brought under control of the central government. Former peasants were confirmed in the possession of lands they had seized from their former lords. Napoleon put France's finances in order—solving the original problem that lead to the Revolution—and stabilized the currency. Social peace was reestablished by allowing exiles and royalists to return to France if they accepted the new regime. Jacobin plots were crushed.

In 1804, Napoleon crowned himself Emperor of France. One foreign visitor who witnessed this event, filled with pomp, was a young Venezuelan, Simón Bolívar, destined to be the liberator of northern South America. What lessons Bolívar drew from that event will be discussed in Chapter 4.

For the first few years the wars went well for France, and Napoleon was popular. Between 1796 and 1809, Napoleon's troops gained victory after victory against the conservative powers of Europe. French armies captured Portugal and Spain. Napoleon put his brother on the throne of Spain, thus displacing the legitimate king of Spain and breaking the previously unbroken thread that had held the Spanish empire in America together since 1492. The result would launch the Spanish American Revolution.

French armies also conquered the Italian peninsula, Austria (three times), Prussia, and Holland. These countries were incorporated into France directly, made into satellites, or neutralized. Napoleon also defeated a Russian army sent against France and was on the verge of invading England. He just couldn't defeat those pesky Haitian slaves.

Napoleon's defeat at the naval Battle of Trafalgar off the coast of Spain in 1805 ended his chances of invading England. Coalitions against France came and went, but the English were always an enemy. The British basically fought the French without interruption from 1793 to 1815.

Once again, as in the time of John Adams, Americans were caught in the crossfire of a life-and-death struggle between England and France. The Republicans were now in power, first under President Jefferson, then under President Madison. Both European sides continued to prey on American shipping, and the British continued to force Americans into the British navy. Unlike Adams, Madison was unable to resist the pressure for war, leading to the inglorious War of 1812 between the United States and Great Britain. Ironically, the English had given in to American terms, but because of slow communications, America had already declared war. (This was in the quaint days when the United States actually followed the Constitution and voted a formal declaration of war—unlike our recent military adventures.) The only major American victory in the War of 1812 (the British had captured and burned Washington, D.C.), was the Battle of New Orleans, which occurred after the war was over, again as the result of slow communications.

The British supported a Spanish guerrilla war against the French that began in 1808. The term *guerrilla* comes from the Spanish word *guerra,* meaning war. *Guerrilla* refers to a "little" or nonconventional war. This war was echoed in Spanish America by patriots there who first maintained that they were holding Spanish America until the legitimate Spanish king was reinstalled on the throne. Eventually, the Spanish Americans would declare for independence, and the English would help the Spaniards retake their country from France.

By 1810, Napoleon was convinced that Tsar Alexander I of Russia was conspiring against France and would form an alliance with England. In the summer of 1812, a French army of 600,000 invaded Russia and captured Moscow (thereby doing better than Hitler, who only got to the outskirts). The Russians characteristically refused to give in and burned Moscow down around Napoleon. The dreaded Russian winter finished the job, and Napoleon abandoned his troops to their fate. By some estimates, two thirds of the French army died in the Russian winter in retreat from Moscow.

In 1813, the French were defeated at Leipzig by the Russians, Prussians, and Austrians. Occupied Europe was freed of French troops, and Napoleon was forced to abdicate the throne of France. After 23 years, the wars begun by the French Revolution were almost over.

Napoleon had kept his promises to the ex-peasants and middle class of France, but by 1808, his government was on outright dictatorship. Under Napoleon, the French government had been efficient, generally popular, and relatively honest. Men of lesser social backgrounds were free to rise due to merit. On the other hand, political parties were outlawed, the legislature was a rubber stamp, and areas of the French Empire were exploited.

Napoleon was not quite through. He had been exiled to the island of Elba but managed to escape to France. In France he raised an army (he was always capable of doing that). He was finally defeated at the Battle of Waterloo in 1815. This time he was exiled to a miserable rock in the Atlantic, St. Helena, where he died in six years.

France returned to monarchy under Louis XVII, the brother of the last king. The king issued a constitution and ruled as a limited constitutional monarch. Absolutism could not be reimposed in France; the French Revolution had thoroughly destroyed the basis of the old regime.

The conservative powers that had defeated France met at the Congress of Vienna in 1815 and established a balance of power that lasted until the First World War in

1914. They could not, however, put the revolutionary genie back in the bottle, nor really restore the old order. In 1848, a revolutionary wave broke out in Europe that, although repressed, would prefigure the Second Age of Revolutions that began in México in 1910, continued in Russia in 1917, extended to China in 1949, and may have culminated in Cuba in 1959.

A Social Revolution: Off With Their Heads!

The French Revolution began as a revolt against taxes, as the American Revolution had. It soon exceeded the American Revolution in violence. While the American Revolution was a political one in which a colony threw off the mother country and then preserved the dominance of the American aristocrats, the French Revolution was an undeniably social one in which the king and nobles lost the basis of their power—and very often, their lives.

The French Revolution, unlike the other three revolutions treated in this book, is the only one that arose in the cradle of Old Europe. The American, Haitian, and Spanish American Revolutions were successful attempts by colonies to throw off the yokes of their mother countries. The French Revolution more thoroughly changed its society than any but the Haitian Revolution. Once the remnants of the feudal system were overthrown, the Church tamed, and the idea of a constitutional monarchy abandoned (largely through the faults of Louis XVI himself), government without a king was suddenly a real possibility. The model was, of course, the American Revolution, so admired by educated Europeans.

As a social upheaval, the French Revolution tried to remake the entire society, not just the governmental system. Thus, the calendar was changed, the metric system was devised, and attempts were even made to create an entirely new religion of state. The French Revolution, in turn, greatly affected events in the United States, directly in the case of the development of political parties and indirectly in the Louisiana Purchase and the War of 1812. The ideas of liberty, equality, and fraternity could not be confined to France but also infected the most unlikely and unintended recipients, the beaten-down slaves of Haiti. The French invasion of Spain led to the Spanish American Revolutions.

The French Revolution lost its way in an orgy of violence and paranoia known as the Terror. How much more fortunate Americans were to have accomplished a "mild" revolution, confined to political, not social, change. This mild political revolution in America led in turn to a gradual social one. The French Revolution is the "granddaddy" of later social revolutions such as the Mexican in 1910 and the Russian in 1917.

The Social Pyramid after the French Revolution

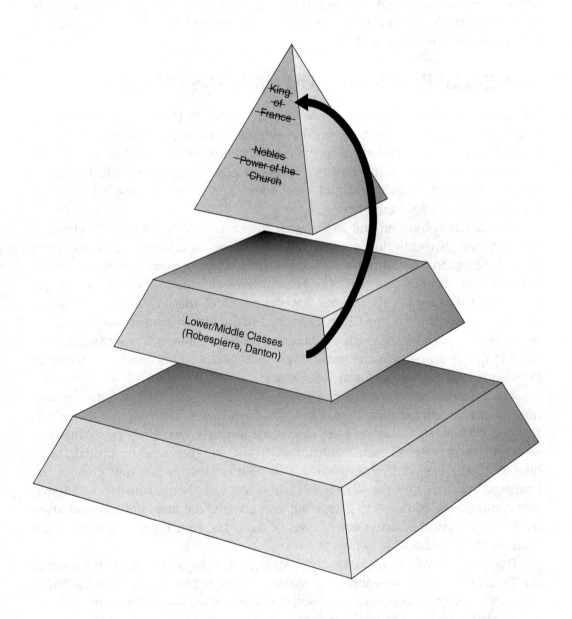

Name: _____ Date: _____

Class: _____

Questions for Reflection and Review

1. How was the French Revolution similar to the American Revolution, and how was it different? What was the spark for the revolution? What climate of ideas contributed to revolutionary ideology?

_____

_____

_____

_____

_____

_____

2. What was the importance of the position of the Catholic Church during the French Revolution? How did the revolutionaries attempt to address their differences with the Church? Do you think that actions taken by the revolutionaries against the Church were helpful or hurtful in gaining support for the revolution? How did the role of religion vary between the French and American Revolutions?

 — the importance of the position of the Catholic Church during the french Revolution was majority of the land was owned by the church, & since the church was exempted from paying taxes

_____

_____

3. The French Revolution lead to a blood bath referred to as the Terror. Which types of people were likely to lose their heads? Why do you think the American Revolution avoided a similar bloodbath?

_____

_____

_____

_____

_____

_____

3 The Haitian Revolution

*The Forgotten, Bloody,
and Cautionary Revolution*

The Haitian Social Pyramid before the Revolution

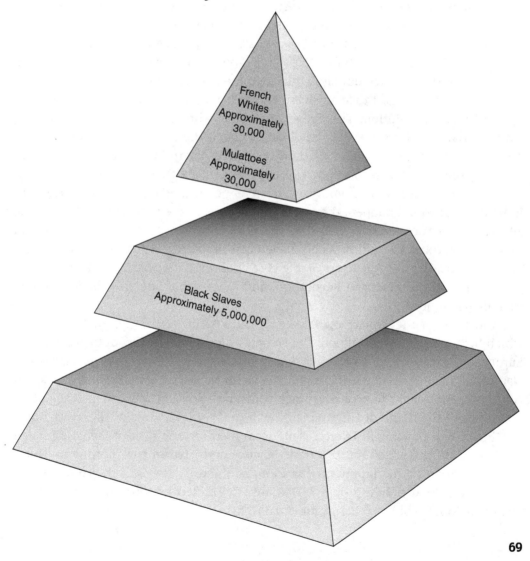

French
Whites
Approximately
30,000

Mulattoes
Approximately
30,000

Black Slaves
Approximately 5,000,000

Why This Revolution Is Forgotten and Why It Should Not Be Forgotten

The Haitian Revolution has never received the importance from historians and the general public that it deserves. Historically, its results were fully as important as those of the American, French, and Spanish American Revolutions. It had tremendous ramifications in U.S. history. It had great impact on shaping the slave system in the United States. As a result of the successful and bloody revolt of Haitian slaves, slave owners in the United States supervised their slaves much more closely, and manumission was made more difficult. Arguably, the slaves' lot became much worse because of the fear of masters that they would end up slaughtered by a slave rebellion, as the French were in Haiti. Napoleon's loss of Haiti caused him to decide to sell all of Louisiana, which doubled the size of the United States.

For similar reasons, the Spanish American Revolutions were greatly influenced by the Haitian Revolution. The Creole aristocrats who led independence accepted aid from Haiti (and, in the case of Bolívar, declared the end of slavery because of a promise made to the president of Haiti) but were determined not to let independence become a social revolution. The large underclass that the Creole aristocrats feared was not black slaves, who were relatively of less economic importance, but Indians. What would happen, they asked themselves, if the Indians in México, Perú, and elsewhere successfully rebelled as the blacks in Haiti had done? The Spanish American aristocrats would probably have been murdered as the French had been. Therefore, the Spanish American Creole elite consciously set out to make a political revolution, like the American Revolution, and not a social one, like the French and Haitian Revolutions.

And what of the impact on France of the loss of its colony, St. Dominique, which became Haiti? Not only did the French suffer the ignominy of being the only European colonial power to lose its colony to a slave rebellion, but the slaves beat Napoleon's troops—the best in Europe! The Haitians also defeated English and Spanish troops who sought to take advantage of the situation in Haiti and took the other two thirds of the island of Hispaniola away from Spain. The loss of Haiti was a devastating economic blow to France. Haiti accounted for one fifth of France's foreign trade, and 40 percent of France's trade balance consisted of transporting and processing sugar and other products from Haiti. In the early stages of the French Revolution, the second richest group of Haitians, the mulattoes, offered to pay off the French national debt in exchange for equal rights.

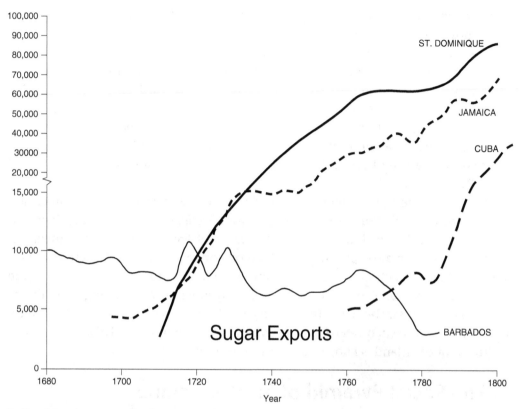

St. Dominique's sugar production surpassed that of other European Caribbean colonies before the Haitian Revolution.

If the Haitian Revolution was so important, how can we explain the fact that it has been so slighted by historians and the general public? There are several reasons, the first of which is economic. Because Haiti today is the poorest country in the Western Hemisphere, the assumption is that it must have always been poor. I hope that the statistics provided in the accompanying graph lay that misconception to rest. Remember that England had debated taking the tiny French Island of Guadeloupe instead of Canada as its prize for winning the French and Indian Wars. That's how much fabulous wealth these small Caribbean islands produced at the time.

Another reason that the Haitian Revolution is not properly appreciated is ignorance about the great leader of the struggle, Toussaint L'ouverture. He should command the same level of respect and admiration enjoyed by George Washington, Simón Bolívar, and Jose de San Martin. Although self-taught he was the intellectual equal of the other liberators. Toussaint was a match for Napoleon as a military man—in fact, he beat Napoleon's army. In my opinion, Toussaint L'ouverture is one of the most wrongly neglected figures in world history.

There has been a general misunderstanding and lack of knowledge about Haiti, even in the Western Hemisphere. Americans tend to be Eurocentric; that is, they know more about Europe than they do their own backyard—the Western Hemisphere. William Jennings Bryan, Secretary of State under Woodrow Wilson, had to be briefed on the location of Haiti and the language spoken there. Bryan's response was, "deary me, imagine that, N——s speaking French!" This outburst by Bryan occurred on the eve of an American invasion and occupation of Haiti that lasted from 1915 to 1934.

A short note here on the term *Creole.* I have already used it to denote the American-born aristocrats in the Spanish empire (the word is *criollo* in Spanish). Creole is also the language spoken in Haiti, which is a mixture of French and African languages. The term *Creole* can also applied to any kind of a mixed culture, such as that of New Orleans. I have also chosen to use the name *Haiti* to refer to the western half of the island of Hispaniola. The word *Haiti* is an indigenous word meaning "mountainous." It is, of course, the name the country has borne since the successful rebellion of its slaves. The French referred to its colony as St. Dominique. Today the eastern two thirds of the island is known as the Dominican Republic.

▲ The Social Pyramid of St. Dominique

All slave systems are brutal, but the Haitian slave system must have been something exceptionally so. On average, Africans imported to work in the Caribbean lived only about seven years, but slaves imported to work in Haiti lived only four years. Only 5 percent of the slaves imported into Haiti worked as house slaves; 95 percent were bound for the fields. Many Africans attempted to commit suicide on the hellish trip to America; once in Haiti, many continued to try. About 2,500 slaves a year attempted suicide. Slaves only had Sunday off, but the plantation owners reserved the right to cancel the Sunday day of rest if they deemed it necessary. If a slave missed work to go to church, the penalty was thirty lashes. Slaves were called to work in the fields by the ringing of church bells. When the rebellion against the slave owners began, slaves ripped the church bells out of the churches.

There were thousands of fabulously wealthy white slave owners known as the "Big Whites." There were also poor whites, known as "Little Whites." There were about 30,000 mulattoes (offspring of white and black parents), about as many as there were whites. Many of the mulattoes were also wealthy and owned black slaves, but socially they were definitely second-class citizens. Since the independence of

Haiti, the entire political history of the country has been a struggle between blacks and mulattoes for power. Today Haitian mulattoes refer to themselves as "the elite." The pendulum of power in Haiti has swung back and forth between blacks and mulattoes, with mulattoes in power much of the time. When "Papa Doc" Duvalier was in power in the mid-twentieth century, he pushed the ideal of "negritude" and black power. During the U.S. occupation of Haiti from 1915 to 1934, the United States preferred to deal with the mulattoes. All of the occupying U.S. Marines were white, and most were from the South and in favor of segregation. The great underclass in Haiti were the half-million black slaves.

The Haitian Revolution was at least as complex, in terms of interest groups, as the French Revolution. All the different factions had their own agendas and sometimes multiple agendas. "Big Whites," "Little Whites," mulattoes, blacks, and the governments of France, England, and Spain all had their own "axe to grind." Within each faction there were subfactions. Among the French, for instance, Jacobins, Girondins, Reactionaries, "Friends of the Blacks," and many more jockeyed for power in Haiti. Some mulattoes favored the retention of slavery, while others were for its abolition. Not the least measure of Toussaint's brilliance was playing all the factions and countries off against each other to his own advantage.

▲ Vincent Ogé: Do All Share the Rights of Man?

There were many Haitian observers in France during the beginning of the French Revolution. One of these was the mulatto Vincent Ogé. The French Assembly passed the Decree of March 8, 1790, which, although ambiguous, seemed to offer the vote to mulattoes over the age of 25 who met certain property qualifications. Ogé returned to Haiti and requested from the white power structure that mulattoes be granted the same "Rights of Man and the Citizen" as whites. The authorities refused. With a couple hundred followers, Ogé attempted to achieve mulatto rights by force of arms but was defeated. Ogé was then "broken on the wheel," the procedure outlawed by Louis XVI in France, as an example to others. The failure of Ogé's attempt to gain legal equality for mulattoes in Haiti drove most mulattoes into the royalist and anti-revolutionary camp.

A common Haitian saying has it that 90 percent of Haitians are Roman Catholics and 100 percent of Haitians believe in Voodoo. Most accounts of Voodoo focus on its lurid details, such as voodoo dolls and hexes. However, Voodoo is a complete religion of African origins with an admixture of American indigenous elements. It has its own theology and liturgy. It is not surprising, therefore, that the Haitian Revolution was begun by a Voodoo priest.

▲ The Night of Fire: Kill Them All!

On the night of August 22, 1791, during a rite celebrated by the Voodoo priest Dutty Boukman, a slave rebellion broke out that would put most of Northern Haiti to the torch. This event is known as the Night of Fire. Not only did the slaves burn many plantations, but they killed thousands of Frenchmen. The slaves were so angry after years of horrible mistreatment that they slaughtered the French man, woman and child. The French would try militarily until 1804 to stem the revolution and return all black people in Haiti to slavery. Boukman's rebellion eventually fizzled out. He himself was captured and his head displayed on a pike to discourage further slave rebellions. The French would send their largest invasion force in history—30,000-plus soldiers under the command of Napoleon's brother-in-law—to Haiti, and they would still never be able to restore the status quo after Boukman. France would not give up diplomatically on repossessing Haiti until 1840, and even in 1840, it considered launching another invasion.

A free black man who stood aside during the Night of Fire was Toussaint. Then known as Toussaint of Breda, because that is the plantation in Northern Haiti where he lived, he would later be universally known as Toussaint L'ouverture. He acquired "L'ouverture" after a remark by a French general who noted that even when surrounded, Toussaint would always find an opening (*l'ouverture* in French).

Toussaint had been freed by his master and educated by a priest (with his master's permission). Toussaint was devoutly Catholic all his life, only questioning his faith at the very end of his life, when French perfidy caused his capture and death. Toussaint learned Latin from his priest-educator and could read and write French, Spanish, and English. His spoken French, however, was far from perfect, since he, like most Haitian blacks, spoke Creole (the true national language of Haiti—French with an admixture of African and indigenous words). Toussaint made sure that his master and family were safely away from danger before he joined the black rebellion at the age of forty-five. He quickly rose the ranks through his intelligence, education, and quick study of military tactics. Like many of the leaders of all four revolutions studied in this book, Toussaint was also a Freemason. This may seem a contradiction for a devout Catholic, but it was a common occurrence in Catholic countries during the revolutionary period.

Big Whites, Little Whites, Mulattoes, Black Slaves, and French Governors

The Haiti that Toussaint was to liberate was a hornet's nest of conflicting racial, national, and social interests. The white slave holders were divided between republicans who had imbibed Enlightenment ideas (except, of course, abolitionism), believers in constitutional monarchy, and reactionaries who longed for a return to royal absolutism. A further subdivision among white slave holders was between those who wished to remain a colony of France and those who wanted independence for Haiti. Independence had the advantage of possibly relieving the wealthy whites of their personal indebtedness to bankers in France. The interest of all slaveholders in Haiti, including mulattoes, was represented in France by their "lobby," the Club Massiac.

The poor, non-slave-holding whites ("Little Whites") had a different agenda. In general they were in favor of the French Revolutionary concept of "equality," which would have elevated them to equal social and political status with the wealthy whites. One of the biggest concerns of the "Little Whites" was

Portrait of Toussaint
SCHOMBERG CENTER / Art Resource, NY

that, in raising their status to a par with the wealthy whites, they would not elevate the "people of color," referring to mulattoes and blacks alike. The "Little Whites" were often also referred to as "Pompons Rouges" (Red Topknots), as opposed to royalist whites known as "Pompons Blancs" (White Topknots).

The Pompons Blancs were led by Hanus de Jumecourt. De Jumecourt believed that the French Revolution would be defeated and the old regime returned to power in France. His ideas was to "play for time" until order could be restored and the old colonial system and slavery could be put back in place. De Jumecourt sought an alliance of convenience with the mulattoes against the blacks.

Mulattoes had originally hoped for electoral and social equality with whites and to retain their superior social position against the blacks. Mulatto slave holders hoped to hang on to their slaves. At one point the mulattoes actually offered to pay off the French national debt to secure equal rights. After the failure of Vincent Ogé's bid for equality, the mulattoes threw their lot in with those whites who wished to retain the slave system and the socially inferior position of Haitian blacks. The mulattoes were led by André Rigaud. Rigaud raised an army of whites, mulattoes, and blacks that became a force in the south and the west of Haiti and served the interests of the mulattoes. Remember that the initial act of the Haitian Revolution, the Night of Fire, had triumphed only in the north.

The role of French governors and legates varied over time according to the winds blowing from France. When bureaucrats became unpopular, they tended to depart to France (if they were lucky). The French governor at the time of the Night of Fire was DePenyier, an elderly monarchist. He gave way to Governor Blanchelande and then Governor and General Laveaux, who was in power until 1796 and who tried to play a multifaceted game mediating between whites, mulattoes, blacks (represented by Toussaint), and increasingly radical French revolutionary governments. Laveaux also had to deal with invasions of Haiti by both English and Spanish forces. He tended only to have real power in the capital of Port au Prince and in the center of Haiti. The north was under the control of Toussaint and the south under the control of the English army for long stretches of time. Laveaux was closely allied with Rigaud and the mulattoes most of the time and alternately tried to placate or liquidate Toussaint.

After 1796, Laveaux was replaced as French administrator of Haiti by Léger-Félicité Sonthonax. Sonthonax represents the stage of the French Revolution of the ascendency of the Jacobins. Sonthonax was extremely controversial, and most historians have a negative impression of him. He came into conflict with Toussaint over many issues, but one is most symbolic. A white man himself, Sonthonax distrusted the white men of Haiti. He felt that they were all counter-revolutionaries and started his own Reign of Terror in Haiti against whites to break their power. Toussaint strongly disagreed with this policy. Toussaint firmly believed that Haiti needed its entire people: black, white, and mulatto. Although Sonthonax did not originally desire to end slavery in Haiti, events forced his hand. More on Monsieur Sonthonax later.

The Spanish and English governments saw the French Revolution and the slave uprising in Haiti as golden opportunities to increase their own empires in the Caribbean. The Spanish would have liked to regain their hold over the whole island of Hispaniola where Columbus had planted the first permanent colony in the New World. They allied with Toussaint and the blacks, but this was an alliance of convenience for both Toussaint and the Spanish. Eventually, Toussaint broke the Spanish alliance and for good measure liberated the whole island of Hispaniola and incorporated it into Haiti. The English captured the French colonies of Guadeloupe and Martinique, where they rapidly reintroduced slavery. They landed an army in Southern Haiti in 1793 and reinstated slavery there as well (this was before the English abolished the slave trade in 1807). Toussaint ultimately outmaneuvered and outfought the English, as he had done with the Spanish.

At the end of November 1791, news of the Night of Fire reached France. The slave owners, represented by the Club Massiac, begged for an army to be dispatched to their home island. Troops were not dispatched at that time, but the Haitian Assembly meeting in Cap François proclaimed that slavery would forever exist in Haiti. The French Legislative Assembly passed legislation that began to grant equal rights to mulattoes. The strategy was to placate the mulattoes in hope that they would join with the whites in preserving slavery.

The Society of Friends of the Blacks *(Société des amis des Noirs)* was founded in France by mostly white Frenchmen in 1788. It was in reaction to the founding of the Friends of the Blacks that the Club Massiac was founded. The Club Massiac was much more successful in the public relations battle by pointing out the revenues generated by the slave system in Haiti. The Society of Friends of the Blacks lobbied the French National Assembly to eliminate slavery, or at least ameliorate the lot of the slaves, but was unsuccessful and eventually went out of existence in 1793, when the blacks of Haiti achieved de facto abolition by force of arms.

After the Night of Fire, only some parts of northern Haiti had been liberated by the ex-slaves. The "Little Whites" in Port au Prince, the center of Haiti and in the West, were enthusiastic for liberty, equality, and fraternity—except as those rights applied to mulattoes and blacks. They formed their own Jacobin club and erected a statue of Marat. Many went east to join the Spanish army. They hoped to displace the "Big Whites" and become the new ruling class of Haiti. The Little Whites (Pompons Rouge) were led by August Borel, nicknamed "The Land Pirate." The mulattoes were caught between the two classes of whites, with both white groups attempting to use the mulattoes for their own purposes. The British in the south of Haiti formed a tacit alliance with the Big Whites (Pompons Blancs) to continue slavery.

Toussaint joined the bands of ex-slaves led by Biassou and Jean François. Both leaders were quickly in awe of Toussaint. They were impressed by his education, skill with folk remedies for illnesses, horsemanship (he had been in charge of the stables on his owner's estate), and logical mind. Toussaint rose swiftly through the ranks and eventually outshone every leader in Haiti.

From Negotiations to Guerrilla War

Three French envoys had been sent by the revolutionary government to assess the situation in Haiti: Roume, Mirbeck, and Saint-Léger. They advised the Haitian Assembly to hold a meeting with the black leaders. Toussaint was always in favor of negotiations. He negotiated many times with many different groups during the Haitian Revolution. He was always allowed safe passage to and from such meetings. It is

Map of Haiti
Image copyright Martine Oger, 2008. Used under license from Shutterstock, Inc.

probably this experience with negotiations that caused him to eventually let down his guard and be deceitfully captured by the French.

These early negotiations came to nothing, and the war by the blacks continued. After the failure of negotiations, Biassou wanted to kill all his white hostages. Toussaint, who always maintained that whites would be useful in an independent Haiti, persuaded Biassou to agree to an exchange of prisoners. Toussaint wanted to retain the expertise of whites in running the plantations on which Haiti's economy depended.

After the failed negotiations, the black armies continued to attack the large cities, moving from the north into the western part of the island. Toussaint mastered the art of small scale hit-and-run tactics. Toussaint acquired an ardent follower in Jean Jacques Dessalines, destined to help complete the liberation of Haiti and become its first president. Unlike Toussaint, who never engaged in wanton killings and torture, Dessalines reveled in these practices. The worst that can be said of Toussaint is that he did not do enough to restrain Dessalines. Both Dessalines and Biassou seemed to be tongue-tied in Toussaint's presence. They would avert their eyes

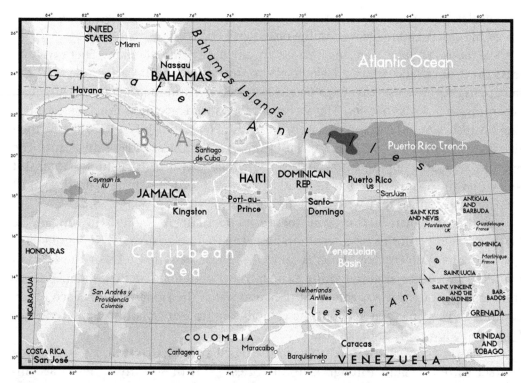

Map of Haiti and the Dominican Republic showing their location in the Caribbean
Image copyright Martine Oger, 2008. Used under license from Shutterstock, Inc.

and always follow Toussaint's directives. Toussaint was now the undisputed leader of black Haitians.

The refusal of most white Haitians to agree to grant rights to the mulattoes caused France to dispatch another set of envoys. There were three of them, but the only one of any importance was Sonthonax. Sonthonax wanted to bring the Jacobin revolution to Haiti gradually. He was convinced that the first group he must win over to advance his agenda was the mulattoes.

When Sonthonax arrived, he was accompanied by six thousand French soldiers and generals Laveaux and Rochambeau. Laveaux was destined to serve as governor. Rochambeau hated blacks and executed every one he captured, although he is best known to Americans for having led the French troops in the American Revolution. Rochambeau wanted to kill all the blacks and mulattoes and restock the Haitian slave system with new slaves imported from Africa. He would leave Haiti only to return later with Napoleon's troops. Laveaux was, on the other hand, an idealist who declared himself in favor of the abolition of slavery. Nevertheless, Laveaux followed his orders and made war on the blacks and Toussaint.

Six thousand men were insufficient to put down the rebellion. There were at least thirty thousand armed blacks in the countryside, and in a guerrilla war, the occupying force must have two to three times the numbers of the insurgents, according to today's theories. The slaves' weapons were acquired from the Spanish. The Spanish would officially declare war on the French on July 9, 1793, and then the Spanish army itself would enter Haiti from the Dominican side of the island. The Spanish were still hoping to reconquer the whole island of Hispaniola. Toussaint knew that the Spaniards would not outlaw slavery, but he used the Spanish against the French as long as they were useful to him.

Sonthonax's plan was to bring the Terror to Haiti. As soon as he landed, he began to build platforms from which to hang the Haitian aristocrats. He founded his own Jacobin Club in Cap François and closed the Jacobin Clubs of the Haitian whites. Sonthonax was also fighting against those whites who desired independence from France. Toussaint was able to sit back and watch the French destroy each other. Sonthonax was only able to hold the capital, Port au Prince, a bit of the center of Haiti, and a few ports in the north.

For a while Laveaux seemed to have the rebellion under control. He even made contact with Toussaint through Catholic priests, but these early contacts accomplished nothing. Laveaux at this point considered Toussaint a traitor, since he was cooperating with the Spanish. The French were startled when blacks went into battle singing the *Marseillaise,* the French Revolutionary anthem (and later the national anthem of France).

No sooner, however, did Port au Prince seem subdued for France, then a new insurrection was launched by Borel and the "Little Whites." His forces lynched both mulattoes and blacks. Blanchelande the Governor was relieved of duty by Sonthonax and replaced by Laveaux. Blanchelande was sent back to France and executed during the Terror on Sonthonax's recommendation.

However, the Convention in France had its own candidate for Governor, François Galbaud. Sonthonax immediately expelled Galbaud. Several weeks later, Galbaud returned with an army of five thousand men recruited in the Caribbean from among exiled monarchists, slave owners, liberated prisoners, and sailors.

In an incident known as "The Leopard" (the origin of this term is unclear), Galbaud landed his troops in Cap François, causing Sonthonax to flee. Regardless of the origin of the term, "The Leopard's" intent was to reinstate slavery, return mulattoes to second-class citizenship, and gain the independence of Haiti from France. At first, Galbaud and the Leopard were successful. They captured Cap François and began an orgy of killing blacks and mulattoes. Unfortunately for the Leopard, the soldiers and sailors found the city's store of rum and other alcohol and quickly became rip-roaring drunk.

Laveaux's advice to Sonthonax was to appeal to the blacks for help in recapturing Cap Francois. Sonthonax had to promise the abolition of slavery to secure the help of the blacks. Thus, Sonthonax was forced by circumstances to end slavery in the northern part of Haiti, which had never been his intent. The revolutionary government in France would outlaw slavery in Haiti, but that was repealed by Napoleon. What really mattered, however, was the situation on the ground in Haiti regarding slavery—and not laws passed in France. Infighting among Frenchmen continued to favor Toussaint and the blacks of Haiti.

Thousands of ex-slaves rolled into Cap François in a successful counterattack against the drunk French. Galbaud himself just managed to escape, although with a huge amount of booty that circulated for years in the Caribbean and North America. Galbaud later died in Napoleon's Egyptian campaign.

In the south of Haiti the "Big Whites" appealed to England for help. The English landed troops in northern Haitian ports such as Môle Saint Nicolás, as well as in the south. (The unfounded fear that Germany might try to seize Môle Saint Nicolás was the United States' rationale for the occupation of Haiti by American forces, which began in 1915 and did not end until 1934.) The English immediately reinstated slavery in the areas they occupied. On June 1, 1794, the English captured the capital, Port au Prince.

The English army occupying southern Haiti began to come down immediately with yellow fever. By the time the English were defeated by Toussaint, they would lose more than twenty thousand men to war and disease.

Sonthonax and Toussaint worked together on and off against the common enemies of Haiti. They both attempted to use each other, but in the end Toussaint was the successful partner. Toussaint's guerrilla tactics became better and better. He had stashes of supplies buried all over the island. French generals remarked that Toussaint's troops were more disciplined than the French. Toussaint enjoyed "good press" in France. This would last until Sonthonax returned to France and began to spread anti-Toussaint propaganda. When Napoleon came to power, he detested Toussaint, which was then reflected in the Napoleonic press. But in the years 1795 to 1798, Toussaint enjoyed a favorable reputation both in the Caribbean and in the mother country.

Toussaint always wanted to reinstate the large estates, which had been the basis of Haiti's wealth. To accomplish this, he needed the knowledge, which only whites possessed at this time, on how to run the plantations. Although Toussaint everywhere abolished slavery, it did not follow that he wanted to allow the ex-slaves to fall into idleness. He enforced labor contracts, whereby the ex-slaves, now free workers, were bound to labor on plantations for a fixed period of time. This recalls nothing so much as the "Black Codes" imposed on newly freed African Americans after the Civil War in the southern United States. Under Toussaint's scheme, if the former plantation holders would return, they would receive one third of the revenue from their plantations. One third would go to the ex-slaves as wages and the remaining third to the Haitian state. Ironically, rich whites with restored plantations came to adore Toussaint!

The United States sold arms to Toussaint as a countermeasure to either France or England becoming too dominant in the Caribbean. While the Americans were selling arms to Toussaint, they were worried about possible spreading slave rebellions that might ultimately reach the United States. Although the Americans and Europeans always feared that Toussaint was trying to export rebellion, the actual situation was that he was too tied down in the situation in Haiti to even think about extending freedom anywhere else but in his country and the rest of Hispaniola.

With the aid of Toussaint, the Spanish were now on the verge of taking all of Haiti, except the southern area held by England. It was at this point in January 1794, that Toussaint broke his alliance with the Spanish and went over to the French side. Part of the reason was Sonthonax's proclamation of the abolition of slavery in northern Haiti. Despite Spanish whispers that Sonthonax's proclamation had not been ratified in France, Toussaint was always a French patriot and never would have allowed the Spanish to take over the island. There was also a widespread rumor, believed by blacks in Haiti, that Louis XVI had intended to end slavery in Haiti when he was captured and imprisoned by the "bad mob" in Paris. The fact that this rumor was false did not diminish its power in Haiti. Haitian royalists repeated it in an attempt to bring blacks over to their side.

Before the Spanish learned that Toussaint had switched sides, he invited the Spanish generals to celebrate a mass with him. The Spanish were completely convinced of Toussaint's good intentions, since he was famous as a devout Catholic. Toussaint's men surrounded the church and slaughtered the Spanish military leadership of Hispaniola after mass let out. Toussaint's solders then cleared the rest of Haiti of the Spanish presence.

▲ The End of Slavery, but No End of War

Slavery in Haiti was finally abolished by the French Convention on February 4, 1794. But in December 1799 Napoleon came to power. He would reinstate slavery in

Haiti and other French possessions. Napoleon revealed his true racial feelings by barring mulattoes and blacks from anywhere from entering France. Napoleon hated black people in general and Toussaint in particular, as would soon become apparent.

Before Napoleon's attack on Haiti and Toussaint, Laveaux had confirmed Toussaint as a general in the French army and provided him with a smart set of uniforms and revolutionary songbooks for his troops. This caused the mulattoes to be jealous of Toussaint's recognition.

Toussaint next turned his attention to the English troops occupying southern Haiti. Toussaint spread the news to slaves in southern Haiti of the abolition of slavery, hoping they would rise against the English. Toussaint took the southern plantations from the owners but protected the whites from the ex-slaves. The former owners would now receive one third of the profits, in accordance with Toussaint's scheme employed elsewhere, of a third of the profits each for the whites, the ex-slaves, and the Haitian state.

In addition to their holdings in the south, the British had enclaves in the center and north of Haiti. In all these areas Toussaint had spies and sappers who undermined the English war effort. The Treaty of Basel granted all of Hispaniola to France. In the topsy-turvy world of European alliances, the English and Spanish now joined forces to try to hold on to a portion of the island against a resurgent France and Toussaint.

The British did not easily give up on Haiti. They launched two new military expeditions from Jamaica. Despite their aversion to Toussaint, the mulattoes piled on against the English. Toussaint suggested to Laveaux an attack on the Spanish forces in the east of the island, to prevent their aid to the English. The governor denied permission for this attack based on the fact that the Spanish were now technically allied with the French. It would take five more years before Toussaint would be able to claim the whole island for Haiti and France.

The mulattoes, under a leader named Vilatte, attempted a coup against Laveaux in Cap François. But blacks counterattacked and within a day had rescued Laveaux. Toussaint then sent his forces to occupy Cap François. Laveaux was so grateful to Toussaint that he elevated him to brigadier general and placed all French troops under his command. Toussaint had become the undisputed master of Haiti.

Unfortunately at this point Sonthonax returned from France, where he had barely escaped becoming a victim of the Terror. As bad as the return of Sonthonax was for Toussaint's moment of triumph, the racist general Rochambeau also returned with Sonthonax. Toussaint resolved to get rid of all the French who were his rivals for power in Haiti. Cunningly he got the Haitian Assembly to elect Laveaux to the Council of Elders and Sonthonax to Council of the Five Hundred in

France. Laveaux left Haiti willingly to take up his new position in France, but Sonthonax stalled.

Sonthonax, in opposition to Toussaint's policy, renewed his campaign to rid Haiti of whites. Toussaint called Sonthonax on his misguided policy and asked, once all the whites in Haiti had been killed, "What would your honor the Commissioner then advise me to do with you?" In an attempt to ingratiate himself with the mulattoes, Sonthonax fired Rochambeau and married his own mulatto mistress.

Toussaint began to win a large number of battles against the English. During these campaigns, Sonthonax continued to push Toussaint to kill all the whites and Toussaint continued to refuse to do so. Toussaint offered to resign as military commander, knowing that Sonthonax could not afford to lose him. The offer was, of course, refused. Toussaint then spread the rumor that Sonthonax was about to reintroduce slavery and declared martial law in Haiti. Sonthonax could not rescind this order since he had just reconfirmed Toussaint as commander. Sonthonax was placed on a ship bound for France. Toussaint had eliminated his French rivals for control of Haiti.

Raids by Toussaint and yellow fever were taking a tremendous toll on the British soldiers. The blacks now began to defeat the English not only in hit-and-run raids but in set piece battles. In April 1798, Toussaint liberated Port au Prince from the British. Wealthy white planters who had recently supported the English now cheered for Toussaint. The British agreed to evacuate their troops from Haiti in exchange for free trade. Toussaint had defeated the English.

The French Directory dispatched Gabriel Marie Theodore, Count of Hédouville, to rein in Toussaint. Hédouville had bloodily repressed revolts in the Vendée region of France for the revolutionary government. Despite being warned by French officials on the ground in Haiti not to underestimate Toussaint, Hédouville proceeded to do just that with a plan to play the mulattoes off against Toussaint.

Hédouville set up a conference with Toussaint. When Toussaint arrived, Hédouville and his staff treated him with barely disguised racist contempt. They attempted to convince him to go to France, but Toussaint refused. Another meeting was called, this time including Rigaud, the mulatto leader. Toussaint offered his resignation as general, and Rigaud felt obliged to do the same. Hédouville was not in a strong enough position to oust Toussaint and did not accept his resignation. Rigaud's resignation, however, was accepted. Toussaint was now free of the last major mulatto leader—for the moment. Rigaud, however, lingered in Haiti long enough to incite a civil war between the mulattoes and blacks. Rigaud finally left Haiti in 1800 but would attempt a comeback, returning with the French army in 1802.

Toussaint decided to use the British and Americans as a counterweight to Hédouville. He opened Haitian ports, which quickly filled up with American and English ships and returned a measure of prosperity to Haiti. When Hédouville protested the British and American treaties, these countries made it clear to Héduoville that they regarded Toussaint, not Hédouville, as the true representative of Haiti.

Hédouville, like Sonthonax before him, wanted to eliminate all the whites in Haiti not considered sufficiently revolutionary. He also attempted to assassinate Toussaint, but the attempt failed. Toussaint's lenient policy toward whites had induced several thousand planters to return to Haiti, and they were firmly in favor of Toussaint and opposed to Hédouville, who appeared, like Sonthonax, to want to kill them. Hédouville then fired blacks from the army and increased the wages of the remaining troops in Cap François. In response, Toussaint spread the rumor that Hédouville wanted to reinstate slavery. The sacked soldiers besieged the port, and Hédouville had to scamper back to France. Toussaint had outmaneuvered Hédouville.

The new nominal French governor of Haiti, Roume, decided to convene a peace conference between the blacks, represented by Toussaint, and Rigaud, still at this point representing the mulattoes (although no longer nominally a general). The talks came to nothing, but it is important to stress the number of times Toussaint entered into peace talks. It was always his preference to negotiate rather than fight. Toussaint's comfort with attending peace conferences would eventually be his downfall, but that was still in the future.

The War of the Knives

The next phase of the Haitian struggle is known as the War of the Knives. It was a civil war between blacks and mulattoes. Rigaud, the mulatto leader, had fought in the American Revolution (yet another reminder of the close relationship between all these contemporary revolutions). Rigaud had slaughtered both whites and blacks while he commanded forces in central Haiti. Before Hédouville departed, Hédouville had sent a communication to Rigaud in which he encouraged him to rebel against Toussaint. A military contest then ensued in which both the blacks and mulattoes committed many atrocities against each other. Governor-Commissioner Roume declared Rigaud an outlaw.

The climactic battle of the War of the Knives took place in the port city of Jacmel. The mulattoes were trapped in the city between the fleets of Toussaint's new allies, the Americans and British. Toussaint's soldiers besieged the port from the land. Riguad was mentally incapacitated during the siege, and the true mulatto hero

Alexandre Pétion
Mulatto hero of the Siege of Jacmel and
friend and patron to Simón Bolívar and the
South American Revolutions
(Library of Congress)

of the engagement was Alexandre Pétion, who was destined to be the President of Haiti and who aided Bolívar and the South American Revolutions. Toussaint eventually prevailed at Jacmel, and Rigaud and Pétion escaped to Cuba and then went on to France. Rigaud gained an audience with Napoleon where he vented his hatred of Toussaint. This reinforced Napoleon's hatred for Toussaint, who was, by this time in some circles, being referred to as "The Black Napoleon."

With the mulattoes defeated, Toussaint could now turn his attention to his long-dreamed-of conquest of the rest of the island and the freeing of the slaves in Santo Domingo. Toussaint requested permission from Roume to invade what today is the Dominican Republic. Roume at first refused but then relented when he was roughed up by some of Toussaint's men. Toussaint first tried to negotiate with the Spanish Governor-General of Santo Domingo. Don Joaquín García replied that he was already being supervised by representatives of France. (The eastern part of the island had technically passed to the French by treaty, but the local administration was being run by the Spanish—not unlike the situation during World War II in the areas of Vichy France, nominally controlled by the French, but supervised by the Germans. See the movie *Casablanca* for an idea as to how such an arrangement worked.) Attempts to establish Toussaint's control of the whole island without bloodshed collapsed with the failure of these negotiations.

Roume then tried to rescind his permission to invade eastern Hispaniola. Toussaint imprisoned Roume with instructions not to mistreat him this time. Roume became ill and Toussaint allowed him to return to France. On October 1, 1800, Spain officially ceded Louisiana to France. Napoleon's dream of an American empire based on Haiti and Louisiana meant that Toussaint was now squarely in Napoleon's crosshairs.

Napoleon sent a letter ordering Toussaint not to invade Santo Domingo, but Toussaint had already left on the campaign and the letter never caught up to him before he had conquered the whole island. On January 1, 1801, Toussaint entered the capital, Santo Domingo. He had become the master of all of Hispaniola. He proceeded to free fifteen thousand slaves, and slavery was abolished on the whole island for the first time since Columbus arrived and started enslaving Indians.

A month after Toussaint captured Santo Domingo, Napoleon began preparations for an invasion of the island. Napoleon supposedly swore that he would not rest as long as an epaulette remained on the shoulder of any black general (although he probably didn't use the term *black*).

Toussaint knew from his spies that Napoleon's army was coming. He hoped to play the French off against the British, as the tactic of divide and conquer had worked so well for him so many times in the past. Toussaint issued a constitution for Haiti in the summer of 1801. What he had in mind was local autonomy for Haiti but within some type of a commonwealth framework with France. Toussaint then sent a letter to Napoleon in which he asked Napoleon to confirm his position as a general in the French army and governor of Haiti. Napoleon had no intention of doing so; in fact, he felt he had to do away with Toussaint to "block forever the march of blacks in the world."

Toussaint's constitution for Haiti had been drafted by a committee of nine, including six whites and three mulattoes. The composition of this committee reflects the fact that Toussaint wanted to reconcile all the races in Haiti and that he felt the expertise of the whites and mulattoes was greatly needed to help Haiti advance.

The constitution was draconian, but in Toussaint's defense, it is important to understand the situation in Haiti when the document was promulgated. About nine in ten blacks could not read or write. Some hundred thousand people had been killed during the revolution, and the economy was in shambles. It seemed that only a strong man could stay on top of the situation. Also, Toussaint had observed how economically inefficient small holdings were in contrast to large plantations. Toussaint was convinced that only big plantations would bring the economic prosperity that the new nation needed.

All administrative power was vested in Toussaint for life, and he had the right to name his successor. All laborers—black, white, and mulatto—had to have a labor contract that bound them to a particular plantation or workshop, usually for six months, or be arrested for vagrancy. The similarity to the "Black Codes" imposed on African Americans in the south after the American Civil War are striking, except this time they were being imposed by a black leader, not white people. The constitution enshrined Toussaint's "program of thirds": one third of the profit for the plantation owner, one third for the workers, and one third for the Haitian state. The system was overseen by Toussaint's military officers. One reason for maintaining a strong army was that Toussaint knew Napoleon's invasion was coming. Nevertheless, when the invasion came in 1802, Haiti's economy was reviving.

⩙ The World Turned Upside Down: Toussaint Beats Napoleon

Napoleon's choice to lead the invasion was his brother-in-law Charles Victoire-Emmanuel LeClerc, one of his ablest generals who had been very effective in the Italian campaign. LeClerc was married to Napoleon's second youngest sister Pauline, who had once worked in a brothel and was infamous as a nymphomaniac. This was to be the largest overseas force ever assembled by France to that time. More than eighty ships with 35,000 soldiers set out to overthrow Toussaint. Later, an additional 80,000 reinforcements would be sent.

A motley cast of discredited former planters, psychotic killers, disgraced politicians, and haters of blacks accompanied the expedition. The Club Massiac had convinced Napoleon that only the reinstatement of slavery would revive Haiti. The mulattoes Pétion, Rigaud, Boyer, and Vilatte readied themselves to resume their positions in Haiti. Racist general Rochambeau was back (and would actually engage in hand to hand combat with Toussaint at one point). Stanislas Féron, a former lover of Pauline Bonaparte, was appointed Deputy Prefect of Haiti. Féron had slaughtered thousands in Marseilles and Toulon during the Terror in southern France. Napoleon had not considered Féron a proper marriage match for Pauline and paired her with LeClerc instead. These were the people Napoleon dispatched to "restore civilization" to Haiti.

Toussaint ordered a policy of burning the large cities, rather than leaving them to the French. The French immediately began an indiscriminate massacre the moment they came ashore. Toussaint's troops faded into the interior where their leader had established an elaborate system of defensive positions and supply caches. Toussaint hoped that between his guerrilla tactics and the spread of yellow fever among the Europeans, he would be able to overcome the French as he had the English before them.

The larger and better equipped French army quickly captured all the important port cities, some of which had been put to the torch by Toussaint's orders. But the blacks fought back so fiercely that LeClerc immediately started requesting reinforcements from Napoleon. He never ceased requesting reinforcements until his death. A couple months after the invasion, one of Toussaint's most important generals, Henri Christophe, defected to the French. He would not be the last such important defector.

General Rochambeau had orders from Napoleon to "destroy all blacks. They are the cause of our misfortune." He was only too happy to comply. Napoleon ordered that all white women who had sexual relations with blacks were to be transported to France where they would be employed as prostitutes. This was in contrast with Toussaint's policies that always insisted on modesty for women; he was even uncomfortable with the feminine fashions of the day, which emphasized décolleté. Toussaint also insisted on marriage for blacks, who as slaves had never been permitted to marry. The French found Toussaint's arrangements for administering the plantations so effective that they left them in place, practically unchanged.

Toussaint won the Battle of Serpent's Ravine, where he trapped Rochambeau and actually briefly fought "mano a mano" with the French General. This victory, however, was counterbalanced by the loss of the Battle of Crête à Pierrot by Dessalines and the defection by Christophe. Another of Toussaint's generals, Maurepas, was forced to surrender to the French. Nevertheless, Toussaint was able to launch a brilliantly successful offensive along the Artibonite River.

Toussaint was approaching the age of sixty by this time and was in declining health. He had trouble with his hips, which caused him to ride in an awkward, but effective, manner. He had no upper teeth and his remaining lower teeth were quite painful.

The French were not faring much better.

Jean-Jacques Dessalines
First ruler of Independent Haiti as Emperor Jacques I
© Bettmann/CORBIS

Five thousand of LeClerc's men had died, and a like number were disabled by wounds or disease. Foreign troops and those infused with revolutionary ardor were disillusioned to find that they were fighting a war of extermination against the Haitians. A large group of Polish soldiers defected to Toussaint's side and went on to lead distinguished lives in post-war Haiti. Yellow fever was predictably beginning to kill a large number of French troops and eventually killed LeClerc himself. Toussaint hoped that by keeping his forces in the field, continuing his hit-and-run tactics and pretending a willingness to negotiate, he could outlast the French until yellow fever could do its awful work.

Accordingly, Toussaint agreed to negotiate with LeClerc at Cap François. It was agreed that all blacks in Haiti would continue in freedom, all black generals and officers would continue in their positions and be integrated into the French army, and Toussaint would be allowed to retire to a plantation he would own and where he would not be molested by the French. Toussaint's reasons for agreeing to this arrangement are not clear. Was he simply worn out and hoping for some peace in his final years, or was he playing for time until yellow fever had laid the French so low that he could begin a final decisive offensive? We will never know, since Toussaint was soon captured by deceit and hijacked to France where he died in a dank dungeon in a little over a year. The French, English, Spanish, and his other enemies were never able to defeat Toussaint militarily, but the French did succeed in liquidating him via treachery.

Pauline Bonaparte expressed the viewpoint of the French once they believed they had neutralized Toussaint, "Now the whip can be used again on the blacks." The French, of course, had no intention of keeping their promises to Toussaint to leave blacks in freedom. They intended to reinstate slavery. But Toussaint was too important a symbol to blacks, even retired on a plantation. Under the pretext of discussing implementation of the peace agreement, the French lured Toussaint into a trap, where he was captured. (Toussaint's wife had a premonition and begged him not to go.) To understand how Toussaint fell for this ruse, it is important to recall the number of times he had attended negotiations with his enemies and received safe passage back home. Various French administrators, mulatto enemies, the English, and the Spanish all kept their words and played by the rules. Only Napoleon's minions resorted to treachery. Nevertheless, the capture of Toussaint would prove to be a Pyrrhic victory for the French.

In July 1802, the ship carrying Toussaint arrived in France. He was taken to the mountain fortress of Fort Joux in the Jura Mountain range. He was fed very little and housed in a damp cell where the temperatures were often below freezing. He was basically held incommunicado but did compose letters to Napoleon demanding to know why he was being treated in such fashion. The "white Toussaint," as he was sometimes called to his great disgust, never responded. By holding Toussaint in such conditions, the French were basically murdering him without having to take responsibility for doing so. Toussaint died April 7, 1803. Thus ended the life of one of the most remarkable and wrongfully neglected men in history.

I hope that this slim volume may contribute in some small way to knowledge about, and appreciation of, Toussaint L'ouverture.

Meanwhile back in Haiti, things were not going well for France. If Napoleon thought that by his treacherous murder of Toussaint he had tamed Haiti, he was sadly mistaken. On July 16, 1802, slavery was restored on Guadeloupe. Blacks rightly assumed that the same would happen in Haiti, and they also assumed, correctly, that Toussaint would be murdered in France.

Even black leaders who had gone over to the French now rose in continuance of the Haitian Revolution. In October 1802 Dessalines, now known as "The Tiger," was back in the field at the head of black revolutionary armies. More than half of LeClerc's troops had died, and he continued to beseech Napoleon for reinforcements. His troops had dwindled to fewer than ten thousand men who were in any condition to fight. He only controlled four port cities and none of the interior. In early November, LeClerc died of yellow fever at the age of thirty and was succeeded as lead general by Rochambeau.

Rochambeau was finally free to loose his full homicidal hatred against Haiti's blacks. He had the black general Maurepas, who had surrendered to the French, and Maurepas's wife tortured and killed in front of their children. Rochambeau had special bloodhounds brought in from Cuba to hunt down blacks. He killed as many blacks as he could.

In July 1803, France was back at war with England. The English blockaded the few remaining ports held by the French, and the French were caught between the British on the sea and the blacks in the interior of Haiti. In 1803, Rochambeau, not surprisingly, chose to surrender to the English and would ultimately die in Napoleon's invasion of Russia.

In 1804 Dessalines proclaimed the independent Republic of Haiti. Only four thousand whites remained in Haiti. Dessalines vowed to kill all of them. In contrast to Toussaint's constitution, Dessalines's did not allow for whites to live in Haiti. There is no doubt that Haiti would have been better off under Toussaint's liberal racial policies. Despite the ongoing European war, French, British, and American ships evacuated the few whites lucky enough to escape from "The Tiger."

When the news reached Haiti that Napoleon had crowned himself Emperor, Dessalines had himself crowned Emperor Jacques I of Haiti. There were still a few French in Santo Domingo, but Dessalines never managed to dislodge them. The Spanish, now fighting on the French side, reoccupied Santo Domingo in 1809. Dessalines governed by terror and divided the plantations among his followers. Afraid of the example of a slave country successfully throwing off the mother country, the United States, France, and England began an economically destructive boycott of Haiti (similar in its results to the U.S. economic boycott of Cuba today).

Henri Christophe and Alexandre Pétion began to intrigue against Dessalines and finally brought him down in 1806. Christophe became president in 1807, but conflicts between Christophe's black followers and Pétion's mulatto allies dogged the new regime. Finally an agreement was reached to allow Christophe to rule as king in northern Haiti and Pétion to rule as president in the south. This split mirrors the perennial battle for power up to this day in Haiti between blacks and mulattoes. Pétion would become an important figure in the Spanish American Revolutions by sheltering Simón Bolívar when he was on the run from Spanish royal troops. Pétion provided shelter, arms, and men for Bolívar's revolution; in return, Bolívar promised to abolish slavery in Venezuela, which he did.

◣ A Social Revolution: The Only Slave Colony to Triumph

The Haitian Revolution is one of the most thorough social revolutions in history. It destroyed the French ruling class and eliminated slavery. In fact it is the only example in history of a slave rebellion overthrowing a colonial power. As such, it was extremely influential with all slaves who hoped to secure their freedom in many parts of the world. The Haitian Revolution profoundly terrorized the conservative colonial countries and slave owners everywhere.

The American Revolution had begun the age of revolutions. The Frenchmen, Haitians, and Spanish Americans who had fought in this first revolution imbibed its lessons. The American Revolution's emphasis on self-determination and the natural rights of men soon spread to Enlightenment Europe and helped inspire the next great revolution, the French. However, the American founding fathers managed to contain their revolution to one that established self-determination by white men; it did not become a social revolution that would free slaves and elevate the status of women and Indians.

By comparison, the French Revolution spun out of control and became a bloody upending of the old regime in France, elevating the lower and middle classes to power. The power bases of the nobles and the Church were destroyed forever, never to be revived. Although a reaction eventually set in, the social revolution in France destroyed the old order once and for all.

It was inevitable that the French Revolution would affect its colony, St. Dominique. Not only were Haitians present in France during the Revolution, but they absorbed the belief in "liberty, equality, and fraternity" propounded by French revolutionaries. The problem was that France had no intention of extending these "rights of man" to their colonists. This was tragically evident when Vincent Ogé returned to Haiti from France. He merely tried to get the Haitian power structure to extend rights to mulattoes, rights that he felt had been extended by the France Assembly. The result was Ogé's execution, and the subsequent bloody, long struggle for Haitian independence, and the abolition of slavery. Only a handful of the most liberal Frenchmen conceived of the abolition of slavery. Even the so-called Society of Friends of the Blacks, was willing to settle for the amelioration of the slaves' conditions.

Even liberal Enlightenment thinkers such as Voltaire conceived of black people as scarcely human. Pauline Bonaparte, before she left for Haiti where she took blacks as lovers, inquired if the blacks in Haiti were not like "insects." Extreme racists like Napoleon and Rochambeau were sure they knew how to solve the "Haitian problem"—kill all the blacks and reinstate the slave system with new shipments of Africans.

In the midst of this racist worldview, a man emerged who belied all the stereotypes about blacks—Toussaint L'ouverture. Despite years spent as a slave, Toussaint made the most of the opportunities that were presented to him. When his master freed him and made a priest available to educate him, Toussaint learned not only Latin but English and Spanish for good measure. Having no formal military training Toussaint soon became the equal, even the superior, of formally trained European generals. Change comes about in history when the right person arrives in the right set of circumstances. Toussaint was obviously the right man to lead Haitian independence. His racially tolerant policies put all his contemporaries to shame.

There can be no doubt that the Haitian Revolution was a social one. The wealthy French planters were removed from their perch on the top of the Haitian social pyramid, and the mulattoes and blacks took over. Slavery was ended. We should not let recent events in Haiti obscure what a remarkable achievement the revolution was. Haiti today is the poorest country in the Western Hemisphere, but it certainly wasn't in 1791. Nor did it have to become such an economic failure after independence.

There are several historical reasons for the sad state of Haiti today, some internal and some external. Internally, after the death of Toussaint and his enlightened racial policies, the struggle between mulattoes and blacks sapped a great deal of energy that could have been devoted to building up the country. Also, Dessalines's policy of killing all whites deprived the country of much-needed expertise. Today the mulattoes, with no irony intended, refer to themselves as "The Elite," as if an admixture of "white" blood makes them superior to the blacks.

However, the external factors in Haiti's decline are more important than these internal squabbles. First of all, the economic boycott slapped on Haiti by the British, French, and United Sates was devastating to the young nation. This partly reflected fear of the spreading "contagion" of slave revolts. It also, quite frankly, marked a "sour grapes" reaction to "inferior" blacks besting white Europeans. Also, the slash-and-burn method of agriculture, started by the French plantation owners and continued by the Haitians, has deforested what was one of the most densely forested countries in the world. Haiti today is an ecological disaster area.

The U.S. occupation of Haiti from 1915 to 1935 is also a major reason for Haiti's poor situation today. The United States entered Haiti partly on the false premise that if it did not seize Haiti, Germany would. The "advisor" who convinced President Wilson and Secretary of State William Jennings Bryan of this patent absurdity was a banker who managed to win for his own bank the concession of administering Haiti's customs revenues and foreign debt, although Haiti had never defaulted on its foreign debt.

The occupation of Haiti was carried out by the U.S. Marine Corps, an all-white force, the majority of whose officers and men hailed from the segregated south. You can image how disastrous race relations were with a segregationist occupying army installed in a black country. Nor is U.S. policy toward Haiti any more enlightened today. Any refugee from Castro's Cuba who touches U.S. soil is immediately granted entry to the country. Haitians who arrive under the same circumstances are deported.

The other major failure of the U.S. intervention was in its stated desire to form a professional "nonpartisan" military in Haiti, which would stay out of politics. This idea also failed in Nicaragua, where the Somoza family dictatorship ruled with the use of the professional "nonpartisan" force for many years. The same thing happened in the Dominican Republic with the long-term dictatorship of Trujillo after an American occupation. "Papa Doc" Duvalier, long-time black dictator of Haiti in the mid-twentieth century, set up his own police force, the "Tonton Macoutes" ("Bogeymen"), and ruled partly on his reputation as a practitioner of Voodoo. Foreign countries did not cause all of Haiti's problems, but they certainly did not help the nation and its people.

▲ How the United States Acquired Louisiana and Held Its Slaves Ever Closer

The Haitian revolution was to have profound repercussions in France, which suffered a huge economic and psychological blow from the loss of its richest colony. Napoleon became so distraught that he gave up his idea of an American empire and sold Louisiana to the United States. In fact, in retrospect Napoleon recognized his folly: "My greatest mistake was to try to subdue Haiti by force of arms. I should have let Toussaint L'ouverture rule it."

Slave holders in the United States were deeply alarmed by the implications of the Haitian Revolution. They cited it as justification for holding their slaves even tighter and making manumission even more difficult. The Haitian Revolution, along with the invention of the cotton gin, may have been responsible for ending some Americans' dreams of the gradual elimination of slavery. Only a bloody civil war could resolve the issue of slavery in the United States.

⬥ The Spanish American Creoles and the "Lesson" of Haiti

Both Haiti and Napoleon would become important players in the next great revolution—in Spanish America. Napoleon's invasion of Spain created the spark for the revolution, and Haiti, by providing sanctuary for its leaders and arms and ammunition, furnished fuel for it. But the Haitian Revolution also functioned as a cautionary tale for the Spanish Creole leaders. They were determined that their revolutionary independence from Spain would not become a social revolution like that of Haiti. The great indigenous underclass in Spanish America must not be allowed to rise, as Haitian blacks had.

The Spanish American revolutionaries having observed both models of revolution—the social and the political—were determined to keep theirs strictly political. The revolution's model was to be the United States, not France, and especially not Haiti. The Creoles succeeded in their political revolution, but not before being given a scare in México, where a Haitian-style social revolution almost triumphed and the Mexican Toussaint emerged in the unlikely guise of a white Catholic priest.

The Social Pyramid after the Haitian Revolution

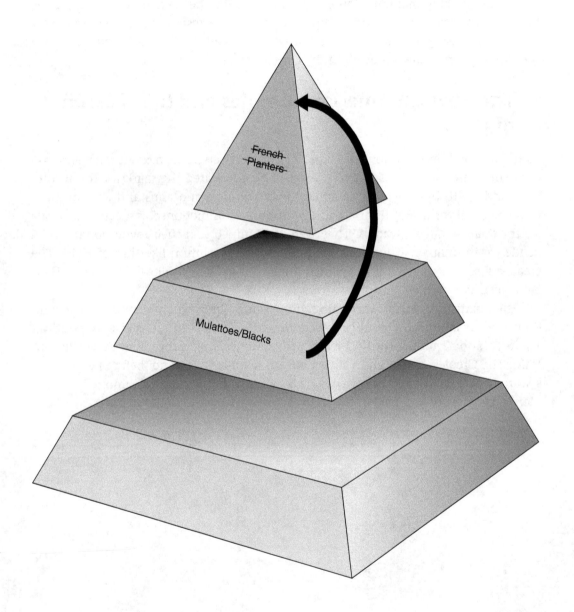

Name: _____ Date: _____

Class: _____

Questions for Reflection and Review

1. Were you aware of the Haitian Revolution before you read this book? Why did you think so few members of the public are aware of this major upheaval? What were the implications for the United States, France, and the wider world of the Haitian Revolution?

_____

_____

_____

_____

_____

2. French revolutionary ideas quickly spread to France's colony St. Dominique. Were all (or even many) Frenchmen willing to extend liberty, equality, and fraternity to all Haitians? Why do you think there was a double standard regarding the rights of Frenchmen and the rights of colonists?

_____

_____

_____

_____

_____

3. Toussaint L'ouverture was one of the outstanding figures of his time. What were some of Toussaint's outstanding traits? What were his racial policies? Why do you suppose Toussaint is not as famous as George Washington or Simón Bolívar?

_____

_____

_____

_____

_____

_____

4 The Spanish American Revolutions

Inspired by the United States and France, Tempered by Haiti

The Spanish American Social Pyramid before the Revolutions for Independence

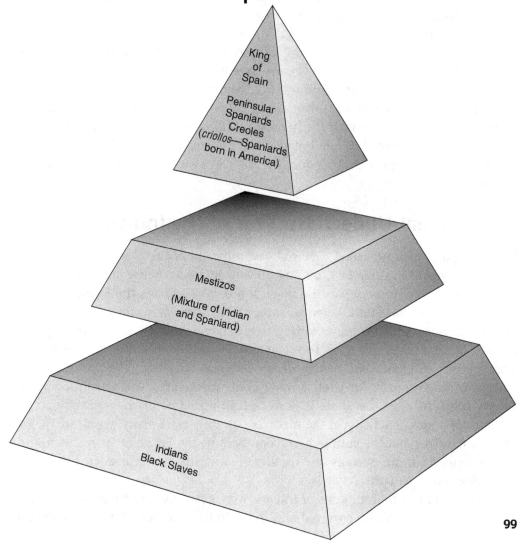

King of Spain

Peninsular Spaniards Creoles (*criollos*—Spaniards born in America)

Mestizos (Mixture of Indian and Spaniard)

Indians Black Slaves

The Glue That Held the Spanish Empire Together

The amazing thing about the Spanish empire in America is not that it eventually fell, but how long it lasted, how large it was, and how wildly successful the Spanish were at instilling their language, culture, and religion on this huge area. No Spanish king ever set foot in the New World, and yet the common thread that kept the empire together was the acknowledgment of all Spaniards in America that the king was the legitimate head of the empire. The event that finally broke the golden thread by which Spain held its American empire was the Napoleonic invasion of Spain and the deposing of the legitimate Spanish king by Napoleon's brother.

The Spanish American elite was composed of two different social classes: the *Peninsulares,* or Spaniards born in Spain, and the Creoles (*criollos* in Spanish). Because of the place of their birth, the Creoles were definitely second-class citizens compared to the Peninsulares. The Creoles were barred from the top positions in the Spanish administration. They could not be viceroys (literally "vice kings," the highest position in the New World). Nor could they usually be members of the royal court, the *audiencia.* In general, the highest position the Creoles could hold was on the *cabildo,* or city council. When independence came, it would be largely led by the Creoles and had a great deal to do with their grievances against the peninsular Spaniards.

The Great Underclass: Fear of the Indian

Those of "pure" Spanish blood were the vast minority of the population in Spanish America. As noted in Chapter 1, one significant difference between the Spanish and English empires in America was the huge numbers of Indians the Spanish encountered in Central and South America. In contrast, there were far fewer Indians in North America. Another major difference between the American and Spanish empires was that very few Spanish women went to the New World. In contrast, a large number of English women came to America. Therefore, the Spanish had to look to Indian women for their female companionship. The Catholic Church quickly began to insist that these liaisons be legitimized by marriage. The result was the birth of a new genetic type, the mestizo. Not only were many people in Spanish America mestizos, but the culture itself soon became a mixture of Spanish and Indians—a mestizo culture. Socially and legally, the mestizos were considered inferior to "pure-blooded" Spaniards.

Despite the fact that millions of Indians were killed by infectious diseases, most notably smallpox, millions survived and today Indians are a majority in Bolivia. In

Perú and México, their numbers were huge in the nineteenth centuries, and they were an important minority population in Guatemala, Venezuela, Colombia, Ecuador, and elsewhere. Indians had very few rights in the Spanish Empire, but at least slavery was outlawed. Nevertheless, they were often held by Spaniards in slave-like conditions. Indians who did not speak Spanish and engaged in a barter economy were basically outside the mainstream of Hispanic culture. In some places they had to pay a head tax just because they were Indians. After the political revolutions that became wars for independence from Spain, Indians remained firmly rooted on the bottom rung of Spanish American society.

Black slavery was not as economically important in the Spanish Empire as it was in North America and Brazil (with the important exception of the Caribbean region), mainly because of a large Indian labor force. The most economically important parts of the Spanish empire were México and Perú, which had large numbers of Indians. Father de las Casas, in trying to save the Indians from slavery, had suggested Africans as an alternative slave labor force, although he later recanted this idea. While blacks were technically on the bottom of the social pyramid in Spanish America, their relative economic unimportance was borne out by the abolition of slavery by the newly independent countries of Central and South America.

◣ The Pyramid Decapitated: Joseph Bonaparte on the Throne

As Napoleon looked south of France's border in 1808, he saw a weakened Spain. He did not have to deal with a monarch of the caliber of Charles III, who had reinvigorated Spain and its empire. Instead Charles IV was a weak and vacillating king. He was completely under the spell of his Prime Minister Manuel Godoy, who was also the queen's lover. Foolish and motivated by greed, Godoy agreed to let a French army pass through Spain to attack Portugal. Napoleon promised Godoy and Spain a portion of the plunder to be achieved when France defeated Portugal. Attacking Portugal was also a way for France to strike at England, since Portugal was traditionally allied to the British. One of the reasons for the traditional Portuguese-English alliance was to preserve Portugal's independence from its larger and more powerful neighbor, Spain.

Napoleon, however, double-crossed Godoy and Spain. He conquered Portugal, and the British put the Portuguese royal family on ships and sent them to Brazil until Portugal could be liberated. Predictably, Napoleon then invaded and conquered Spain.

Charles IV by the Spanish artist Goya
(Library of Congress)

Charles IV, frightened by the French invasion of Spain, abdicated the throne. Spanish patriots, denouncing Charles as a traitor, persuaded his son Ferdinand to ascend the throne as King Ferdinand VII of Spain. Charles tried to reclaim the throne, so that Spain and its American empire had two claimants to the throne. Napoleon invited the father and son to France to resolve their differences and held them under house arrest for the remainder of the French occupation of Spain. (This situation would last until Ferdinand VII returned to the Spanish crown in 1814; Charles IV died earlier.) Napoleon then placed his brother, Joseph Bonaparte, on the Spanish throne. The Spanish refused to recognize Joseph Bonaparte, whom they derisively referred to as "Pepe Botellas" (Pete Bottles), implying that he was a drunk.

The loss of a legitimate king was the one event guaranteed to throw the Spanish empire into chaos. Despite the distance from Spain, despite the fact that the Spanish kings were "absentee landlords," the Spanish empire had always held together based on the agreement that the Spanish king was the "boss." Now there was no legitimate head of the country and its American colonies, and thus Napoleon fired the shots that began the dissolution of the Spanish empire.

The Spaniards refused to accept the French invasion and fought back. Napoleon's troops, however, were the best in Europe, and Spain was a third-rate military power. The Spanish army could not stop Napoleon, and his troops entered the capital, Madrid. The rump Spanish government fled to the south of Spain, at Cádiz. Spaniards resorted to guerrilla war against the French. The term "guerilla war" derives from the Spanish word *guerra* (war). A *guerrilla* is literally a "little," or unconventional war. The Spanish kept French troops pinned down in Spain for seven years in this Peninsular War.

The Spanish "government in exile" in Seville, and later Cádiz, organized itself into a "Junta for the Defense of Ferdinand VII." The idea was that Spanish loyalists would hold Spain and Spanish America "in trust" for Ferdinand VII, until such time as he was back on the Spanish throne. As we shall see, similar Juntas sprung up all over Spanish America.

Despite the fact that the Junta at Cádiz was fighting to put Ferdinand back on the throne, the Junta eventually came into conflict with the "Desired One," as Ferdinand came to be called. The Junta was not immune to French revolutionary ideology, even as it fought the French. Its members were influenced by the whole body of Enlightenment thought and the example of the American Revolution. What the junta wanted was to make Spain a constitutional monarchy. What wasn't clear yet, due to the king's captivity in France, was that Ferdinand wanted to rule as an absolute monarch. Ferdinand's desire to rule as an absolute monarch also had important ramifications in Spain, as we shall see.

The Junta in Spain also claimed to rule the Spanish American colonies, a claim the colonies would ultimately reject. The usurper king, Joseph Bonaparte, made the same claim, which was also rejected by the Americans. Bonaparte sent more than sixty French officials to Spanish America to try to rule there. The Spanish Americans expelled or imprisoned every one of the French envoys. Joseph Bonaparte also tried to get Spaniards to act as his viceroys in México and New Granada, but none was willing to collaborate with the French.

Influenced by American and French revolutionary ideas, the *Cortes,* or parliament, wrote a liberal Constitution providing for a limited monarchy for Spain. While the Constitution of 1812 declared the colonies to be an integral part of Spain, it did not give the colonies the right to trade with any country but Spain. The Junta at Cádiz that called the Cortes included some Spanish American Creoles who were disappointed with these restrictions as they had imbibed the Enlightenment concept of free trade. The only participants who were happy with this trade limitation were the peninsular Spaniards who held the monopoly concessions, especially those in Perú. Despite allowing a few Creoles to participate, the Junta at Cádiz did little regarding America, except to demand money to fight Napoleon. Spanish Americans felt little or no loyalty to the Cádiz Junta. Most Spaniards in America felt the Cádiz Junta was a poor substitute for the king.

Although most Creoles were not ready for independence from Spain in 1812, Spanish power had declined throughout America in recent years. There were armed revolts in 1808 and 1809 against Spanish troops still in America to protect the viceroys. Some of these revolts paradoxically declared independence while still proclaiming their loyalty to Ferdinand VII. Bogotá, Caracas, and Valladolid, México, had revolutionary movements under local Juntas for the defense of Ferdinand VII. The leaders of these Juntas claimed that if the Spanish city of Cádiz could set up an interim ruling Junta, so could they. Not knowing what Ferdinand VII thought (he was still imprisoned in France), the American Juntas proclaimed for Ferdinand VII and against the Cádiz Junta.

Finally, in 1814, with the support of the English army under the Duke of Wellington, the Spanish forced Joseph Bonaparte off the throne and restored Ferdinand VII. Showing little gratitude for the sacrifices made by the Cádiz Junta in his name, Ferdinand had members of the Junta imprisoned and revoked the Constitution of Cádiz. Ferdinand intended to rule as an absolute monarch. Liberals in Spain were unhappy with Ferdinand, and there were many revolts in Spain against the king.

The most important revolt in Spain against Ferdinand's absolute monarchy occurred in Spain in 1820. This is called the *Riego Revolt*. Rafael del Riego was a Spanish military officer and Freemason who led Spanish troops who were going to be sent to Spanish America to put down patriot revolts against Spain. Instead of leading these troops against America, Riego refused to allow them to get on the ships and instead used the soldiers to start a rebellion against Ferdinand's absolutism. Ferdinand was forced to accept the Constitution of Cádiz written in 1812 and to rule as a limited monarch.

In many ways the Riego Revolt was the most important event aiding Spanish American independence since Napoleon's invasion. The revolt had two significant effects. First, it cut off reinforcements to America and allowed the patriot armies to triumph. Second, and perhaps most important, it swung conservative Creole thinking in favor of independence because the conservatives believed that Spain was now in the hands of "dangerous liberals." In fact, as we shall see, some of the conservative Creoles would invite Ferdinand VII to come to México, where they would allow him to rule as an absolute monarch. Ferdinand declined the invitation, but conservatives in México would not give up on the concept of a European prince ruling over México until their disastrous experience with importing Maximilian of Austria in the mid-nineteenth century. The Riego revolt was deeply symbolic for the Spanish psyche, as evidenced by the adoption of the Spanish Republican troops of the "Hymn of Riego" as their battle song during the Spanish Civil War of 1936–1939.

◣ The Hymn of Riego

Serene and happy, brave and daring,
Let us sing, soldiers, the battle hymn.
Our voices shall astonish the world
Which will see us as the children of the Cid.
    Soldiers, the country calls us to the fight.
We swear to her to conquer or to die.
Never saw the world more noble daring,

Nor any day when greater valour was shown,
Than that when excited we saw the fire of battle
Awaken in Riego the love of his land.
    Soldiers, the country calls us to the fight.
We swear to her to conquer or to die.
The war trumpet echoes to the winds;
Affrighting the greedy, the cannon now roars.
Our warrior daring calls forth the audacity
And the ingenuity of our nation.
    Soldiers, the country calls us to the fight.
    We swear to her to conquer or to die.

Spanish American patriots achieved many military victories from 1820 through 1823. Spain could not aid its forces in America because of internal struggles. Finally in 1823, France and Austria invaded Spain and restored Ferdinand as an absolute and reactionary monarch. But it was too late for Spain to retake its American empire.

México was the one place in Spanish America where a social, rather than a political revolution, almost triumphed. México is also anomalous in Spanish American independence in two other ways. It is the only country in which the revolt for independence started in the provinces and not in the capital city. It is also the only Spanish American country where a Creole leader set out to consciously start a social revolution and not a political one. In fact, the early Mexican revolution for independence became a cautionary tale for other Creole leaders, as did the Haitian Revolution.

When news reached México that Napoleon had captured the Spanish king and placed his brother on the throne, the Creoles of the *cabildo* begged Viceroy Iturrigaray to form a junta for the defense of Ferdinand VII. The viceroy vacillated and the peninsulares replaced him with their own man, Gariby. Since México City was unwilling to establish a junta, the Creoles of the provincial town of Valladolid established their own junta for the defense of Ferdinand VII.

▲ Father Hidalgo and the Failed Social Revolution

The unlikely first leader of Mexican independence was a Catholic priest, Father Miguel Hidalgo y Costilla, the parish priest of the poor regional town of Dolores. Hidalgo was a Creole, the son of a poor farmer. He was educated at the Colegio de San Nicolás in Morelia. He later became the president of this institution and was

Father Miguel Hidalgo y Costilla, leader of the abortive Mexican social revolution and precursor of Mexican independence, as painted by the Mexican muralist Clemente Orozco

(Library of Congress)

known for his scholarship, good works, and empathy for the lower classes in México, the mestizos and Indians. He was an ordained priest who served in several different parishes.

By 1800, however, Hidalgo had acquired a bad reputation with the authorities. He read Enlightenment literature, which was on the Catholic Church's index of banned works. Despite being banned by the church, Spanish American aristocrats had wide access to the writings of Voltaire, Rousseau, and other Enlightenment writers as well as religious books critical of the church. Hidalgo had spoken favorably of the French Revolution and seemed to question the virgin birth. He fathered two daughters, which was not unheard of for a priest at this time, but Hidalgo scandalized the church authorities by acknowledging them as his daughters. Hidalgo was denounced to the Inquisition. He was also accused of speaking disparagingly of the Pope and making his church a meeting place for spreading radical ideas. The church authorities decided to deal with Hidalgo by sending him to some back-water village where they thought he couldn't cause any trouble.

Father Hidalgo was popular in his new post in the tiny village of Dolores. He studied Indian languages and continued to read radical literature. He helped the Indians improve their vineyards, planted mulberry trees for the cultivation of silk worms, and operated a brickyard, tannery, and pottery works. He also formed an orchestra for the Indians. Father Hidalgo was well loved by his parishioners, Indians and mestizos alike.

Hidalgo was involved in politics with a special vocation for helping the under-dogs of society, the Indians and mestizos. He became impatient with the slow devel-opment of Mexican patriotism among the Creole elite. In 1810 a conspiracy for independence was formed in nearby Queretaro, and Hidalgo, naturally, joined. This conspiracy involved many prominent Creoles and even the Spanish official in charge of Indian affairs, known as the *Corregidor*.

On Sunday morning September 16, 1810, news reached Hidalgo that the Spanish authorities had uncovered the plot. Hidalgo had to choose whether to flee to escape capture or proceed with the insurrection. Father Hidalgo chose to start the movement that would eventually lead to the independence of México from Spain. He rang the church bells and summoned the citizens of Dolores to the church. He told them that a new dispensation had come to them that day and asked them whether they were willing to accept independence. He appealed to the Indians by asking them if they would be willing to start the effort to retrieve their land that had been taken by the hated Spaniards three hundred years ago.

Hidalgo released prisoners from the jail and began arming a ragtag group of Indians, mestizos, and a few Creoles. For the most part his "army" was armed with machetes, knives, and sticks. Their battle cries were "Long live our Lady of Guadalupe, death to bad government, and death to the *Gauchupines*" ("the spurred ones," a derisive term for Spaniards).

This was the *Grito* (Shout) of Dolores, which to this day is celebrated as Mexican Independence Day (not Cinco de Mayo, as many Americans mistakenly believe, which is the celebration of a victory by the Mexican army over a foreign army during the French intervention of the nineteenth century). Even though the revolution that Father Hidalgo started was not ultimately successful, the radical priest better represents the aspirations of the majority of the Mexican people than the wealthy Creole who ultimately brought independence. Father Hidalgo is considered a hero in Mexican history, whereas the author of independence, Augustin de Iturbide, is not. Father Hidalgo intended to lead a social revolution that would have elevated the Indian and the mestizo. Instead, México's revolution of independence from Spain was a political revolution, like that of the United States, which left mestizos and Indians on the bottom of the social pyramid.

It is important to distinguish between the independence revolution of 1810 and the event that began in 1910, which is better known in history as "The Mexican Revolution." The earlier revolution ended up bringing about political change, while the one starting in 1910 was a social revolution. Neither revolution was quick or easy. The revolution started by Hidalgo began in 1810 and ended in 1821. The "shooting" part of the 1910 revolution did not end until 1920. The Mexican Revolution of 1910 was one of the major events of modern history and predated the equally important Russian Revolution by seven years.

Symbolism and religion were important in Mexican independence. Father Hidalgo's Indians and mestizos marched under the banner of the Virgin of Guadalupe. It is impossible to underestimate the importance of the Virgin of Guadalupe in México. She is the symbol of Mexican nationalism. Guadalupe is a dark-skinned virgin who looks like a mestizo or Indian. The origin of the Virgin of Guadalupe in Spain is interesting. During the Spanish Reconquest (711–1492), in which the Christians retook Spain from the Moslems, the little Spanish town of Guadalupe in western Spain went back and forth several times between the Christians and the Moslems. Once when the Muslims were about to take the town, the Christians buried the statue, which depicted the virgin as light-skinned. Once the Christians retook the town, they dug up the statue and the virgin's skin color had changed to dark. The Spaniards during the war of Mexican independence carried a banner of a light-skinned virgin. Thus there were "dueling virgins" during the war, each carrying a heavy charge of symbolism.

Father Hidalgo's army quickly picked up followers, mainly Indians, in the towns through which it marched. Eventually Hidalgo's army had 50,000 to 60,000 men, a huge army for the times. To call it an "army," however, is an exaggeration. It was really a large, armed mob.

Wealthy Creoles, even those who favored independence, were alarmed by this type of army, with its overtones of social revolution. The war shifted focus as Indians and mestizos sought to avenge three hundred years of Spanish misbehavior and injustice in México. When the mob encountered Spaniards, they tended to be slain on the spot. The biggest massacre occurred in the Spanish regional city of Guanajuato. When Hidalgo's army approached Guanajuato, the Spanish Intendent prepared to hold the town. Five hundred Spanish soldiers holed up in the *Alhóndiga de Granadítas* (Royal Granary). Hidalgo's forces captured the city easily, but the Spanish forces still held the granary. Finally, through sheer force of numbers Hidalgo's men overcame the Spanish opposition and the Spaniards were killed to the last man—all five hundred of them. No wonder conservative citizens were frightened of Hidalgo's army. The army also captured Guadalajara, the second largest city in México.

Hidalgo then turned his attention to México City. The city was lightly defended, and Hidalgo could easily have taken it if he had not hesitated. But he did—and we all know what happens to he who hesitates. The reason for Hidalgo's hesitation is not clear, but he may have feared what his mob might do in México City. By not moving immediately on the city, Hidalgo lost the social revolution and, eventually, his life.

Given time, the Spaniards mounted a counterattack on Hidalgo and began to push him out of all the territory he had captured, including Guadalajara. As he fled north, news reached Father Hidalgo that the Junta of Cádiz had declared a pardon for all rebels in Spanish America. Hidalgo was invited to show his loyalty to Ferdinand VII by laying down his arms.

Hidalgo's response to the amnesty offer was to state:

In the discharge of our duties we will *not* lay down our arms until we have wrested the jewel of liberty from the hands of the oppressor. We are resolved to enter into no agreement which does not have for its basis the liberty of the nation, and the enjoyment of those rights which the God of Nature granted all men—rights inalienable which must be sustained by the shedding of rivers of blood if necessary. . . . Pardon, your Excellency is for criminals, not for defenders of their country!

Quoted in Hubert Herring, *A History of Latin America* 1967

We can see clearly in Hidalgo's defiant speech the influence of Enlightenment ideas and the American and French Revolutions ("inalienable rights"). This Catholic priest sounds like a deist ("God of Nature").

After Father Hidalgo was captured, he was supposed to receive the benefits of the ecclesiastical *fuero,* the right to be tried by a church court, even for a violation of civil law. Instead, he was stripped (literally) of his priestly robes and shot by a firing squad on July 31, 1811. The social revolution, the only one with a chance to succeed in Spanish America, died with Father Hidalgo. But Mexican nationalism had its first martyr and hero, one who would not be equaled until Benito Juárez in the later nineteenth century and Emiliano Zapata in the twentieth.

Continuing the Cause

Others attempted to continue Father Hidalgo's work. Jose María Morelos was a mestizo who had become a priest at age 25. Morelos had little education and little intellectual curiosity. Father Morelos had been one of Father Hidalgo's lieutenants. By using guerrilla tactics, Morelos had managed to control most of southern rural México by 1813. In that year, Morelos called a congress at Chilpancingo, which declared México independent and wrote a constitution.

Spanish forces eventually overpowered Morelos's army and captured their leader. Morelos was taken to the prison of the Inquisition in México City. As with Father Hidalgo, he was denied the ecclesiastical fuero, stripped of his priestly robes, and executed by

Jose María Morelos continued the independence movement after the execution of Hidalgo.

© Bettmann/CORBIS

firing squad on December 22, 1815. Morelos's bones lie under the Monument of the Revolution in México City.

The next to step forward to pick up the fallen banner of Mexican independence were Félix Fernandez and Vicente Guerrero. Félix Fernandez, whose nom de guerre was Guadalupe (for the Virgin of Guadalupe) Victoria (for victory), had the perfect name for the revolution. He was destined to become the first president of republican México.

Victoria was the only president of México to finish out his entire term of office in the first half of the nineteenth century. Guerrero, too, was slated to be president—but not to finish his term, due to the instability of early Mexican politics.

Victoria and Guerrero were strong enough to hold the south but never strong enough to defeat the royalist forces. For that to happen, an aristocratic Creole would have to double-cross the Viceroy and ally the royalist troops with Victoria and Guerrero and the cause of independence.

The man who finally brought independence to México, Augustín de Iturbide, is not considered a hero in Mexican history for reasons that will become clear as we tell his story. He brought not the social revolution that Hidalgo wanted to elevate the Indian and mestizo, but rather a political revolution like that of the United States. At the top of the social pyramid, Iturbide replaced the peninsular Spaniards with the Creoles. He replaced Ferdinand VII with himself. The rest of the social pyramid remained the same, with the exception of black slavery, which was ended shortly after independence. Recall that black slavery did not have the same economic importance in México that it did in the American south, Brazil, or the Caribbean islands.

Augustín de Iturbide
He finally brought independence to México but is not considered a hero in Mexican history due to his vainglorious rule and placing a crown on his own head as Emperor Augustin I of México.

(Library of Congress)

In 1820, the liberals in Spain rose against Ferdinand VII in the Riego Revolt. The Spanish liberals forced Ferdinand to convene a parliament and restore the Constitution of Cádiz of 1812. Mexican Creole conservatives felt that they could no longer trust the Spanish government, and the upshot was that wealthy Creole conservatives now swung in favor of independence. Also, a break with Spain would give the Creoles a chance to topple the peninsular Spaniards from the top of the social pyramid and perhaps facilitate a takeover of their business concessions.

Many Mexican conservatives favored establishing an independent kingdom in México. They hoped to persuade Ferdinand VII to escape liberal domination in Spain and come to México, where he would be given a free hand to rule as he pleased. However, Ferdinand declined the offer, preferring to stay in Spain and fight it out with the liberals there. Thus Ferdinand kept in place the tradition of no Spanish king visiting the New World up to that time. Conservatives in México would not be cured of their king fixation until the disastrous experience with Maximilian of Austria in the middle of the century.

Augustín de Iturbide was a wealthy Creole who saw which way the wind was blowing. Iturbide asked the viceroy to appoint him as commander of the royal troops attacking Guerrero. Instead of fighting Guerrero, he joined him, thus double-crossing the viceroy. Guerrero and Iturbide agreed on "Three Guarantees" for México: allegiance to the Catholic Church, a monarchy (preferably under Ferdinand VII), and equality of Creole and peninsular Spaniards. Note that mestizo, black, and Indian citizens were not granted equality. This was a political revolution to place the Creoles in power, not a social one to give equality to all citizens. With the forces of Iturbide and Guerrero combined, they easily took México City on September 27, 1821. It had taken eleven years since Hidalgo's *Grito de Dolores* for México to achieve independence, and in the process the revolution had been turned from a social one to a political change of leadership.

Historians' viewpoints on Iturbide are nearly unanimously unfavorable. Iturbide depended on the Church and the army for his power. The trouble was that after eleven years of warfare, the treasury was bare. Iturbide could not pay his generals. Trouble was predictable.

Since Ferdinand VII would not come to México, Iturbide had himself crowned Emperor Augustín I. México did in fact have an empire. In addition to all the land that then belonged to México, including what is now the U.S. Southwest up to the Oregon border, México also held Central America. What are now the independent countries of Central America—Guatemala, Honduras, El Salvador, Nicaragua, and Costa Rica—were all part of Iturbide's empire. But the area was too vast for México to ultimately control.

Iturbide and his wife–empress tried to rule over a court of ridiculous pomp and splendor. His was supposed to be a limited monarchy but Iturbide was contemptuous of Congress. In 1822, he simply jailed fifty members of Congress who had disagreed with him. In October 1822, he abolished Congress altogether and announced that he would rule by decree.

A crisis was imminent and came from a logical quarter, the army. General Antonio Lopez de Santa Anna, who was destined to be the major power in México for the next half century, rose against Iturbide. To state that Santa Anna was a colorful personality would be a vast understatement. In one of many examples, he first tried to come to power by seeking to marry Iturbide's sixty-year-old sister (when he was twenty-seven); Iturbide refused this offer. In warfare with France (during the "Pastry War," so called because the French landed in México to recover debts owed them, including to a French baker), Santa Anna's leg was shot off. He carried his leg back to México City and invited the diplomatic corps to witness the leg being buried with full military honors. Years later, when Santa Anna was out of favor with the Mexican people, they dug up his leg and dragged it through the streets. A final example came when Santa Anna was in exile in Cuba during the Mexican War with the United States. Santa Anna approached American diplomats and promised that if they slipped him through their blockade of México, he would then surrender México to the United States. When he arrived in México, Santa Anna, of course, raised an army and fought the United States. This is part of the reason why I love history. The things that actually happened are so much wilder than anything that could be made up!

After Santa Anna deposed Iturbide in 1823, México changed its governmental system from a monarchy to a representative republic based upon the example of the United States. This included the concept of federalism and created state governments. This was a departure, since México had always been ruled centrally from México City, going back to the times of the Aztecs.

The concept of a republican government was difficult to achieve. Unlike the United States, upon whose constitution the Mexican constitution was based, Mexicans had no experience in self-government. Americans had been writing their own laws since the founding of the House of Burgesses in 1619, and all thirteen colonies had their own assemblies. Mexican independence had replaced the peninsular elite with the Creole elite. The highest position that a Creole could hold under Spain was town councilman. All major laws had been written in Spain, not in México. Although a few mestizos rose to positions of power after the revolution, the politically active portion of the Mexican population was 20 percent at the peak. Most mestizos and all Indians were denied political input. Therefore, given their differing backgrounds, it is not surprising that the United States experiment in representative government was successful after the revolution and the Mexican attempt was not.

The small minority of politically active citizens in México divided themselves into the Conservative and Liberal Parties. This was the political organization in almost all of the new Spanish American countries. To underscore the importance of freemasonry in the revolutionary era, the Liberals belonged to one lodge of Masonry and the Conservatives to another.

The Conservatives looked to the practices and faith of the past. They supported special privileges for the Church and the military. The conservatives were divided among themselves on only one major issue: monarchy versus a republican form of government. They were centralists who wanted all México governed, as in the days of the viceroy, from México City.

The Liberals favored federalism versus centralism. They were typical nineteenth-century liberals in that they wanted all Mexican citizens to be treated equally by the law (similar to the French revolutionary concept of equality). Thus, they wanted to end the church and military *fueros* (right to be tried in a church or military court, even for civil crimes). With the French revolutionaries, they shared the concept of anti-clericalism. They felt the church was too powerful and wanted secular education, hospitals run by the state and not the church, and civil marriage. They wanted to break up the large estates and church properties and make México a country of small independent farmers, as they conceived the United States to be. The Liberals had some slight social consciousness (the Conservatives had none), and they were willing to admit a small number of successful mestizos into the political elite.

The issues that the Liberals and Conservatives fought over, including in civil wars, were largely unimportant to the average Mexican who was engaged in a daily battle for economic survival. To the vast majority of citizens, the issues that the Conservatives and Liberals clashed over were esoteric. The underclasses would have preferred their leaders to use their energies in reaching practical solutions to economic problems rather than battling over whether education should be secular or religious. The revolution for independence from Spain changed in character, from Father Hidalgo's social crusade for the mestizos and Indians to the political revolution that triumphed with the Creoles fully in control.

The Creoles Channel the Revolution

The South American revolutions for independence from Spain never had the chance to become social revolutions, as the early Mexican revolution might have become. The Creoles were in charge of these revolutions from the very beginning and had no intention of letting the struggle veer off into a social crusade. They had the examples of the American, French and Haitian revolutions before them and consciously picked the United States' political revolution as the example to follow.

The seminal figure in the South American revolutions is Francisco de Miranda, known as "El Précursor" (the precursor to the South American revolutions). Miranda was a wealthy Creole from Venezuela who worked tirelessly for independence. He fought on the side of the patriots in the American Revolution. He also took an active part in the French Revolution, siding with the Girondin faction. He barely escaped death during the Terror. Miranda envisioned an independent new world country that would unite all the former Spanish and Portuguese colonies. He would have called this huge country "Colombia" after Christopher Columbus. Even before the Napoleonic invasion of Spain in 1806, Miranda landed in Venezuela and attempted a revolution. In this he had been aided by the British. This attempt at revolution failed, and Miranda escaped to England where Simón Bolívar would eventually meet him and bring him back to Venezuela for another attempt at independence.

Miranda's critique of the Haitian Revolution is instructive and may be taken as the "official Creole position" on that revolution:

> I must confess to you that as much as I desire liberty and independence for the New World, as much I fear anarchy and [a] revolutionary system. May God won't permit those beautiful territories to have Saint-Domingue's fate, a theatre of bloodshed and crimes, under the excuse to bring liberty; before it would be better for them to remain for yet another century under the barbaric and imbecile Spanish oppression.

> Letter of Miranda to Turnbull,
> *Archivo General de Miranda XIV*, Dec. 16, 1798, p. 207

There can be no clearer statement of the Creole desire for a political revolution like that of the United States rather than a Haitian social-style revolution. Miranda and Bolívar were willing to accept shelter, troops, and monetary support from Haiti, but a revolution to elevate the masses—never!

◢ Bolívar's Campaign for Gran Colombia

Simón Bolívar was the successful liberator of northern South America. Bolívar was a Creole born to wealthy parents in Caracas, Venezuela, on July 24, 1783. Both Bolívar's parents died when he was very young. His early education was received from a tutor, Simón Rodríquez, an ardent follower of the French Enlightenment thinkers, especially Rousseau. At the age of seventeen, Bolívar was sent to Spain for further education. With his wealth and contacts, he moved easily in the circles of the court of Charles IV. At nineteen he married well to a niece of the Marquis of Toro. Bolívar brought his young bride home to Caracas, where she died within a year. Bolívar swore never to marry again, and he never did. He did have many mistresses, including one who became his intellectual and political confidante, Manuela Sáenz. He would meet her many years later during his campaigns in Ecuador and Perú.

After the death of his wife, Bolívar went to Paris and lived the life of a wealthy playboy. He had come into his considerable fortune. But all was not dissipation for Bolívar; he attended several fashionable salons hosted by French society ladies, where he was further introduced to Enlightenment ideas. In 1804, Bolívar witnessed Napoleon putting the crown of France upon his head. Bolívar was impressed by the pomp and circumstance of Napoleon's investiture and used it as a model for the many ceremonial entries into the liberated cities of northern South America. This love of ceremony was quite in contrast to the style of the liberator of southern South American, General Jose de San Martín. In 1805, Bolívar took a trip to Rome with his tutor, Simón Rodríquez. Bolívar had a transcendental experience in Rome, fell to his knees, and swore never to rest until he had liberated his country from Spain.

Simón Bolívar, the Liberator of northern South America
(Library of Congress)

In 1810, the Cabildo of Caracas sent Bolívar to England to bring back Miranda for another attempt at independence. At that time Miranda was sixty and Bolívar twenty-seven. Venezuela declared independence from Spain, but by 1812, things were going badly militarily for the patriot side and Miranda was about to flee the country again with the funds for the revolution. It was at this point that Bolívar suffered the biggest stain on his reputation. He and others turned Miranda over to the Spanish authorities. Bolívar claimed that Miranda was fleeing out of cowardice and stealing the funds for the revolution. The much more likely reason for Miranda's attempted flight was that he was retreating to relaunch the revolution at a more auspicious time, as he had done several times previously. At any rate, turning over Miranda to the Spanish authorities allowed Bolívar to save himself and he was allowed to go into exile. Miranda died in a Spanish prison.

Bolívar stopped briefly on the island of Curaçao before going on to New Granada (Colombia) in 1812. In Bogotá, Bolívar gathered patriot supporters into an army and attacked Venezuela in 1813. He declared "war to the death" to peninsular Spaniards, but this was no social revolution. Bolívar was opposed to the rise of Venezuela's *pardos* (mixed race people), blacks, and Indians as a biproduct of independence. He was willing to use the underclasses in his army, as were the royalists.

The three countires in the upper left of this map of South America, Venezuela, Ecuador, and Colombia, constituted Bolívar's *Gran Colombia*.

(Image copyright Adam Golabek, 2008. Used under license from Shutterstock, Inc.)

He would declare the end of slavery and that all (male) citizens were equal, but his belief was that the Creoles would be the natural leaders of the new countries and be in charge of all the major decisions.

Bolívar did not favor a monarchy (as opposed to Iturbide and San Martín, who did). Bolívar favored a republican form of government with a strong lifetime president who would name his own successor. Bolívar was an astute political analyst, and he understood that there was insufficient experience in self-government in Spanish America for a U.S. style federal political system which he called "overly perfect." The main outline of what Bolívar desired for the new republics is clear: a lifetime president (he was the logical candidate for this position) and an elected congress, which was effectively controlled by the Creole elite.

The struggle for independence in Venezuela and Colombia would be long and hard—as it was in México and all of Spanish America. It would last at least fifteen years, cause thousands of casualties, and wreak havoc upon the economy. Bolívar's attack on the royalists was no more successful than the earlier one he fought in, led by Miranda. By 1815, Bolívar was in exile again in the British colony of Jamaica. In Jamaica he wrote a famous "open letter" describing the patriots' war aims and his analysis of the political system he envisioned. From Jamaica, Bolívar moved on to Haiti. The southern half of Haiti was then under the control of the French-educated mulatto, Alexandre Pétion. Boyer had been aiding the Spanish American patriots in the belief that Haiti would be safer from recolonization if the colonial powers were thrown out of Latin America and slavery outlawed. In Haiti, Bolívar collected supplies and a force of 5,000 men and 250 officers with which to launch his next revolutionary attempt. Bolívar promised Pétion that he would end slavery in Venezuela, and he kept his promise.

Bolívar finally succeeded in his military campaigns in Venezuela during the period 1817–1820. One of the most important reasons for Bolívar's success was his alliance with the *llanero* leader Jose Antonio Páez. The llaneros were tough Venezuelan "cowboys," similar to the gauchos in Argentina. Bolívar decided not to attack the capital, Caracas, until he had control of the countryside. Another factor that led to Bolívar's success in Venezuela was the arrival of 4,000 officers and enlisted men, mostly from the British isles, who came to help fight for the independence of South America. It was to the economic advantage of England to abolish the Spanish monopoly trade system.

In February 1819, Bolívar felt secure enough about the situation in Venezuela to call a congress at Angostura. A constitution was produced that enshrined Bolívar's idea of a strong executive. Even though the war in Venezuela was not completed, Bolívar felt secure enough to take the war to the royalists in Colombia. With 2,000 men, Bolívar won a battle against the royalists at Boyacá in 1819. Bolívar entered Bogotá with the kind of fanfare he had seen Napoleon use to his advantage. Bolívar was proclaimed Liberator and President of New Granada (Colombia). He left Francisco de Paula Santander to rule day to day as vice president. Santander and Bolívar would later come to blows over national sovereignty issues.

In December 1819, Bolívar announced the creation of Gran Colombia. This was his plan to unite Venezuela, Colombia, and Ecuador (which was not yet liberated) into a single nation. The Gran Colombia was always stronger in Bolívar's imagination than in reality. It turned out that the three countries had little desire to be linked together. Santander and Páez began to plot to separate their respective countries, and the Ecuadorians would turn out to feel the same way. Already these infant republics were responding to the pull of what I feel has been the strongest "ism" in world history since the nineteenth century—nationalism. Subsequent history has shown that nationalism trumps socialism, communism, and capitalism. Men can seemingly always be recruited to kill in the name of nationalism.

In 1820, there were still royalists troops to be dealt with in Venezuela. Bolívar was greatly aided by the Riego Revolt in Spain. This revolt stopped the flow of royal troops to Spanish America. It also helped convince conservative Creoles to come out for independence, since Riego forced Ferdinand VII to accept the Constitution of Cádiz and Ferdinand was now under the control of "dangerous liberals" in Spain. Conservative Creoles flocked to Bolívar's banner of independence. Given the military situation, the royalist commander General Morillo was forced to sue for a cease fire. Within two months, Bolívar had broken the cease fire and on June 24, Bolívar defeated the royalists at the battle of Carabobo. This was a decisive battle, although not all royalist troops were finally expelled from Venezuela until 1823.

Bolívar was now anxious to capture Ecuador and make it part of the Gran Colombia. He sent General Jose Antonio Sucre to capture Quito, Ecuador, in May 1822. Bolívar entered Quito with his usual pomp and circumstance.

Unfortunately, the Gran Colombia worked better in Bolivar's imagination than in reality, and Venezuela, Colombia and Ecuador would each soon go their own way.

Letter of Bolívar's Mistress (Manuela Sáenz) to Her Husband (an Englishman):

"No, no, no never again man, so help me heaven. . . . Senor, you are excellent, you are inimitable, I shall never say anything else about you; but you my friend, to leave you for General Bolívar is something; to leave another husband without your qualities would be nothing . . . and do you believe I, after being the beloved of this general for seven years, with the certainty of possessing his heart, would choose to be the wife of the Father, Son, or the Holy Spirit . . . ?

I know I can never be joined to him in what you call honorable love. Do you think me less honored because I am his lover and not his wife? Ah, I do live by the social preoccupations invented for mutual torment. In heaven we shall marry again, but not on earth.

In paradise we shall pass an angelic life, one wholly spiritual, (because as a man you are heavy). Everything there will be in the English manner, since monotonous life is reserved for your people . . . love is arranged for them without pleasure, conversation without grace, the walk is hurried, the salutation without reverence, they get up and sit down with caution, they do not laugh at their own jokes; all these are sacred formalities; but I, miserable mortal, who laugh at myself, at you, at these English seriousnesses, how I shall suffer in heaven . . . as much as if I had to go and live in England or Constantinople. . .

Have I bad taste? Enough of jokes; formally and without laughing . . . I shall tell you that I shall never join myself to you again. . .

That you are an Anglican and I am a pagan is the strongest spiritual obstacle; that I am in love with someone else is still better and stronger. Don't you see with what precision I reason?

Your invariable Friend,

Manuela"

Quoted in Hubert Herring, *A History of Latin America*, 1967

The day he entered Quito, Bolívar met Manuela Sáenz, the woman who was to become his long-time mistress, confidante, and political partner. She would eventually save his life during an assassination attempt. But at this point, we will turn to the efforts of the leader of southern South American independence, José de San Martín. San Martín and Bolívar would eventually link up in Ecuador for a momentous meeting to plan strategy for the final liberation of South America.

The Liberation of Southern South America

In 1810, the Cabildo Abierto (Open Town Council) of Buenos Aires began the process of liberating southern Spanish America. The Argentines had special reasons to resent the Spanish colonial trade laws. Under the concept of mercantilism, Argentina was only permitted to trade with Spain. But like their counterparts in what became the United States, Argentineans engaged in smuggling and unauthorized trade, especially with the English. If the Argentines played by the rules, they would have had to wait for their manufactured goods to be produced in Northern Europe, sent to Spain, then transported to the Caribbean, sent across Panama by mule train (there was no Panama Canal at this point), shipped to Lima, Perú, and sent through Upper Perú (Bolivia) and Paraguay and then to Buenos Aires. Goods then would cost ten times what they had in Spain. The merchants in Lima, who made a nice profit by transshipping these goods, loved the system. This fact helps explain why Perú was the Spanish colony most loyal to the crown during the independence struggle.

In 1806, the English tried to take advantage of the desire of Argentina for free trade by landing an invasion force to seize the territory for themselves. Just because the Argentines wanted free trade didn't mean they wished to become an English colony, and they soon drove the English out. The English tried again in 1807 and again were driven out. One of the most interesting incidents of that war occurred when one of the English ships ran aground, and the Argentines rode their horses right up to the ship to fight the British.

When news reached Argentina of the French usurpation of the Spanish throne, the Argentines formed their own junta for the defense of Ferdinand VII. In 1813, Paraguay declared its independence, not only from Spain but from Argentina. Situated between Argentina and Brazil and always the scene of conflict between the Spanish and Portuguese, Uruguay eventually followed the path of independent nationhood under the gaucho leader José Gervasio Artigas.

Those Argentine Creoles who declared for independence attempted to defeat royalist forces by attacking them at their strongest point, Upper Perú (Bolivia). The reason that the strongest royal forces were located in Upper Perú was to protect the fabulously wealthy silver mine of Potosi. In fact, Upper Perú would be the final Spanish stronghold to fall in the war of independence. The Argentines tried and failed several times in their attempt to take Upper Perú. The Argentines would then turn to a new military commander who had a different strategic plan, José de San Martín.

San Martín was born in 1778 in northern Argentina. His father was a Spanish military officer, and José followed in his footsteps. When San Martín was seven, his family returned to Spain. José entered military service at the age of eleven and eventually reached the rank of lieutenant colonel in the Spanish army. In 1808, when Ferdinand was forced off the Spanish throne, San Martín returned to Argentina. He joined the Lautero Lodge of Freemasons (Bolívar was also a Mason). In 1812, San Martín decided to devote himself to the cause of Argentine independence and offered his military experience to the service of the government of Buenos Aires.

Like many Creoles, San Martín favored a constitutional monarchy form of government for Argentina. San Martín was ordered to attack the royal army in Upper Perú. But he realized that the Argentine forces were too weak to prevail in such a head-on attack. Therefore, pleading imaginary health reasons, San Martín requested the command of a backwater region of Argentina, which bordered the Andes Mountains and Chile. San Martín's plan was to build up his forces and make a daring attack on Chile across the Andes, taking the royalist forces in Chile by surprise and joining pro-independence forces already in Chile. Then San Martín would transport his army by ship and attack Perú, finally joining his forces with those of Bolívar for a final assault on Upper Perú. San Martín's plan succeeded brilliantly, if slowly and with great suffering for his army and for San Martín himself.

José de San Martín, liberator of southern South America. Unlike the flamboyant Bolívar, the more modest San Martín never received the credit due him during his lifetime.

(Library of Congress)

San Martín, unlike Bolívar, thought of himself purely as a military man and did not want to become a politician. After independence, San Martín would leave Argentina precisely to avoid being dragged into political factionalism. However, events would cause San Martín to reluctantly delve into the political arena. One of the first political acts he was called upon to perform was to bring about a united patriot effort in Chile, where the independence cause was divided between those who followed the Carrera brothers and the followers of Bernardo O'Higgins. On February 12, 1817, San Martín's forces defeated the Spanish troops at the Battle of Chacabuco in Chile. In April, San Martín went on to defeat the last remaining royal troops in Chile.

Unlike Bolívar, San Martín refused all honors offered him in Chile. The city of Santiago presented San Martín with 10,000 pesos, which he gave away to a hospital. Chile offered him an expensive set of silver dishes and a salary of 6,000 pesos a year for life, but he refused to accept anything offered him.

In 1820 San Martín was ready to move north to Perú. But he needed a navy to ferry his troops. As fate would have it, a mysteriously cashiered British admiral with a "fleet for hire," Lord Cochrane, volunteered for the job (he would later sell his services to the Brazilians). Cochrane cleared the coast of Perú of Spanish ships and put together a fleet to carry San Martín's forces north.

Perú was a much more difficult campaign than Chile, as San Martín knew it would be. Perú contained many wealthy *peninsulars* and even Creoles who had profited from the Spanish monopoly system and had no desire for change. The patriots could not count on many supporters inside Perú. Instead of attacking Lima, through its port of Callao, San Martín opted for a landing in Pisco.

At this point, the Riego Revolt occurred in Spain. This, of course, cut off royalist reinforcements for Perú. With the prospect of no reinforcements, the viceroy was forced to negotiate with San Martín. However, the discussions came to nothing and the viceroy fled into the interior toward Upper Perú and the Spanish garrison protecting the silver mine at Potosi. As in other parts of Spanish America, some conservative Creoles who felt that Ferdinand VII was now in the hands of "dangerous liberals" turned to supporting independence. They also reasoned that they could wrest control of mining and business from the peninsulares. The Cabildo of Lima invited San Martín to enter the city in July 1821. A week later San Martín declared the independence of Perú.

The independence of Perú, however, was far from won. San Martín only controlled Lima and a small coastal strip. The Spanish controlled the rest of Perú and all of Upper Perú (Bolivia). Lima was full of royalist supporters, waiting for the right moment to rise against San Martín. The royal army was at least twice as big as San Martín's. San Martín was also unable to pay Lord Cochrane for his naval services. Despite his reluctance to assume political office, San Martín decided to take the post of dictator of Perú.

The only way for Perú to be liberated was for San Martín and Bolívar to join forces. On July 26 and 27, 1822, in Guayaquil, Ecuador, the two main liberators of South America met to plan strategy. The toasts offered by both men give great insight into their characters. Bolívar's toast was said to be, "To the two greatest men in South America—General San Martín and myself!" San Martín toasted to the early end of the war and to Bolívar's health. It soon became apparent that the two men could not work together. Even San Martín's offer to serve under Bolívar's command did not satisfy the latter's desire to be the only major leader in the conquest of Perú. In an incredible act of self-denial and sacrifice for the common cause, San Martín turned his army over to Bolívar and went home to Argentina. Unfortunately, San Martín was hounded by various political factions in Argentina to join their parties. Since San Martín despised politics, he went into exile in 1824. Not until 1880 was San Martín finally honored in his native land.

One of the areas of conflict between Bolívar and San Martín had been what system of government a liberated Perú should have. San Martín argued that Perú was not ready for a republican government and that a monarchy under a European prince limited by a constitution would be most practical. Bolívar stated that a monarchy would be contrary to the ideals of the revolution. Although the departure of San Martín freed Bolívar of a perceived rival, he had other problems. Both

Santander in Colombia and Páez in Venezuela wanted to dismember Gran Colombia and lead their respective countries. Even with San Martín's troops, the royalist forces in Perú were still larger than the number of Bolívar's troops. In September 1823, Bolívar entered Lima to a huge celebration. But Bolívar's treasury was bare and there were still many secret royalist sympathizers in Lima waiting for a chance to do him in.

Bolívar sent his most loyal lieutenant, the 29-year-old Jose de Sucre, against the larger Spanish army. On December 9, 1824, at the Battle of Ayacucho, Sucre won the decisive battle that would liberate Perú. Although some cleanup operations were ahead for Bolívar's army, Ayacucho represents the effective end of Spanish resistance in South America. Although Bolívar knew that he would probably return immediately to Bogotá to quell the separatist movements, he was tired and ailing. He stayed on in Lima and overindulged on women, food, and drink. He already had tuberculosis and, despite his dissolute lifestyle, continued to lose weight.

The silver mine at Potosi was finally captured by Bolívar in 1825. Bolívar wanted Upper Perú to remain part of Perú, but Sucre supported its independence. Bolívar was only somewhat mollified when the new country was named Republica Bolívar (now called simply Bolivia) in his honor. Bolívar attempted to fashion a constitution for Perú with a lifetime presidency modeled on the constitution of Gran Colombia. But as soon as Bolívar left Perú, the Peruvians proceeded to modify the constitution, which they felt had been imposed by a "foreigner" (note again the importance of nationalism among all the new republics).

Finally, Bolívar returned to Gran Colombia in 1826, after an absence of five years. His vice president, Santander, was plotting against him, as was Páez in Venezuela. To Bolívar's face, Santander assured him of his loyalty to the Liberator, and then Bolívar hurried off to Venezuela to keep Páez in line. When Bolívar returned to his home in Colombia in September 1828, he was attacked by armed men and saved from assassination only by the quick actions of his mistress, Manuela Sáenz. He spent most of the rest of that night hiding under a bridge.

Bolívar was now very ill and bitter. He resolved to leave South America and go into exile in some European country. Bolívar felt betrayed and that his life had become a torment. He began his trip to the coast of Colombia to take sail for an undisclosed European port. He was so ill, however, that he was never able to make it to the dock and died of tuberculosis on May 8, 1830. He was 47 years old. "America," he wrote, "is ungovernable. Those who have served the revolution have plowed the sea." The Gran Colombia, Bolívar's prize accomplishment, promptly fell apart. Within four months of Bolívar's death, Venezuela, Colombia, and Ecuador went their separate ways.

Brazil Declares Independence from Portugal

It is instructive to contrast the independence of the Spanish American countries from Spain with that of the independence of Brazil from Portugal. Both independence movements had the same proximate cause, the invasion of the Iberian Peninsula by Napoleon. But there the similarities stop. For one thing, Brazilian independence was practically bloodless. The Portuguese, who were virtually a client state of England, followed English instructions and transferred their royal court to Brazil, until such time as the British could liberate Portugal from the French. The sea passage was long and rough, and the ladies of the court came down with lice and had to shave their heads. An undoubtedly apocryphal, but amusing, story is that the Brazilian ladies, believing shaved heads to be the height of Portuguese fashion, shaved their heads too!

After the defeat of the French, the British advised King John VI to return to Portugal. He left his son, Pedro, as regent of Brazil and advised him that if Brazil demanded independence, to grant it, but "keep the crown on your own head." The Portuguese government was now in the hands of "dangerous liberals." Almost exactly mirroring events in neighboring Spain during the Riego Revolt, Portuguese liberals forced a constitution modeled on that of the Cádiz Constitution, limiting the power of the king of Portugal. When the Portuguese parliament insisted that Pedro return to Portugal and vetoed some of his cabinet appointments, Pedro hesitated briefly. He received a thinly veiled message from his wife, "The apple is ripe, pluck it or it will rot." "Fico (I stay)," Pedro proclaimed. He was crowned Emperor Pedro I of the independent country of Brazil. What little bloodshed there was occurred when the Portuguese garrison tried to force Pedro on a ship to Portugal, but a Brazilian mob turned the tables and forced the Portuguese troops on to the ship instead.

In addition to the lack of bloodshed, the other major difference between Spanish American independence and the independence of Brazil was over the issue of slavery. Like the United States, Brazil relied more heavily on slave labor than did the rest of South America. Accordingly, slavery was abolished in Spanish America shortly after independence, while it took a civil war in the United States to abolish it. Slavery in Brazil lingered much longer because of its economic importance. The last two countries in the Western Hemisphere to abolish slavery were Cuba (still a colony of Spain) and then Brazil.

◢ The Western Hemisphere Comes of Age

The United States and Great Britain were two of the first countries to recognize the new Spanish American republics. The United States was happy to see other European colonies throw off their colonial masters (except for Haiti, with its example of slave rebellion). England was quick to recognize the newly independent countries for economic reasons. With the Spanish mercantilist system of restricted trade out of the way, England was the country best situated to profit from trade with the newly independent Spanish American countries. People in the United States are used to the idea of "American" (the term has been expropriated by the United States, but everybody in North and South America is an "American") economic domination of Latin America, but for most of the nineteenth century, England's commerce dominated.

Accordingly, England invited the United States to issue a joint declaration that the former Spanish colonies were off limits to European recolonization. England did not need to dominate Spanish America politically during the nineteenth century when it could dominate economically. Even though the young United States did not have the military power to back up such a doctrine (and England had the navy to do so), the United States decided to issue the doctrine on its own. After all, England was one of the European powers that had been "booted out" of the New World. Even though the United States issued the doctrine alone, England was happy to enforce it with its fleet, since profits from trading in the Western Hemisphere were so great.

The statement issued by the United States telling Europeans not to try and recolonize the Western Hemisphere is, of course, the famous (and infamous) "Monroe Doctrine." Despite the fact that President Monroe issued the doctrine in 1823 and it bears his name, it was actually written by his Secretary of State, John Quincy Adams. At first the Monroe Doctrine was strictly a defensive statement that "Europeans stay out of American affairs." But as time went on, American presidents expanded the Monroe Doctrine so that it became an offensive doctrine asserting American power in the Western Hemisphere. In fact to most Latin Americans, the Monroe Doctrine has become an *offensive* doctrine. By the end of the nineteenth century, the United States was making statements such as, "The United States is practically sovereign in this Hemisphere," and "Our fiat [word] is law." The doctrine was extended to make the Caribbean an American (U.S.) lake. U.S. interventions in Panama, Nicaragua, México, Haiti, the Dominican Republic, and Cuba demonstrate why Latin Americans find this doctrine offensive.

There is another important point to make here about the history of the Western Hemisphere. This is called "The Western Hemisphere Idea." Americans tend to be Eurocentric—that is, they know more about Europe than they do about anything "south of the border." Even many Spanish American countries are guilty of the same reasoning, looking to Spain and Europe as the "mother country." The Western Hemisphere Idea suggests that this Eurocentrism is misplaced because all Western

Hemisphere countries have a common history and have more in common with each other than with Europe.

How can this be? Consider that, according to the latest scientific consensus, the first "Americans" crossed a land bridge that existed approximately 30,000 years ago linking Asia and Alaska. The first Americans were Asian in origin. This holds true for all of North and South America. The first Americans filtered down from Alaska and settled in North, Central, and South America. The next stage of common American history was European colonization. The Europeans then imported African slaves to almost all parts of the Western Hemisphere. New and unique racial pairings occurred in the Western Hemisphere. One example was the blending of Spanish and "Indian" genes in México to form a new race, mestizos. Finally, the countries of the Western Hemisphere rebelled against their European masters and became independent countries.

Therefore, Americans, or "United Statesians," have more historically in common with, for instance, Argentines, than they do with the English. We should therefore spend much more time studying our common "American" cousins in North and South America than we do studying Europe. I know this will not happen for a number of reasons, including the economic power of Europe, but I would like to see the concept of the Western Hemisphere Idea contemplated a great deal more than it is. Most Americans, for instance, could probably better complete a map of Europe than they could a map of the Western Hemisphere. I can't tell you how discouraging it is when people find out my wife is from Colombia and ask, "What part of México is that?"

The Spanish American Creoles had before them the examples of the American, French, and Haitian Revolutions, when their time for independence came. They consciously chose the American model.

◢ The Pyramid Adjusted but Sustained

The only Creole leader of independence with a desire to elevate the lower classes was Father Hidalgo, and he died a martyr. The Creole who finally triumphed in México was Iturbide and he had no social consciousness. Iturbide and many of the Conservatives in México were monarchists; in fact, Iturbide had himself made Emperor Augustin I. Not until the rise to power of Benito Juárez, a full-blooded Indian, to the presidency of México would Indians receive even a symbolic victory in Mexican politics, and not until the Revolution of 1910 would anything resembling a social revolution occur in México.

The revolution in México, like all four revolutions we have studied, was greatly influenced by Enlightenment ideas. The triumph of these ideas in México is all the more remarkable when you consider that the first attempt to put them into action was by a Catholic priest. The influence of freemasonry is also remarkable in Roman Catholic México. The earliest Mexican political parties, the Liberals and Conservatives, were organized around different Masonic lodges. Even the American and British ambassadors to early independent México got into the Masonic act. The U.S. ambassador joined the liberals' lodge, and the British ambassador joined the conservatives' lodge, as the two diplomats jockeyed for influence in México. The American ambassador Joel Poinsett is also famous for bringing the colorful "Christmas plant"— the poinsettia—to the United States. Bolívar and San Martín in South America were also Masons.

WHITHER?

The Monroe Doctrine
Formulated by John Quincy Adams and President Monroe to keep Europeans from re-colonizing America, the Monroe Doctrine has been abused by American presidents to intervene and bully Latin American governments.
(Library of Congress)

A Political Revolution: The Creoles in Charge

The South American revolutions for independence never had a chance of becoming social revolutions. South American Creoles were far too close geographically and emotionally to the Haitian Revolution to wish such a fate for their countries. "The Precursor" of South American independence, Francisco de Miranda, stated that he would prefer to remain under Spanish rule for a hundred years rather than have a Haitian-style social revolution, and Bolívar and San Martín agreed. The underclass that the Creoles especially feared was not black slaves, who were not that economically important on the mainland, but Indians. The Creoles had long experience with Indian revolts, such as that of Tupac Amaru, and knew the potentially explosive consequences for the ruling classes if such revolts succeeded. Thus even though the Creoles accepted aid from Haiti and abolished slavery, a new Haitian Revolution was to be avoided at all cost.

It is most useful to think of the Spanish American revolutions for independence from Spain as a contest between peninsular Spaniards and Creoles. Both sides were willing to use Indians, mestizos, and pardos (the Venezuelan term for mulattoes) in their ranks, but there was no question of elevating the social standing of these groups after independence.

In fact, the very conservative cast of Creole leadership is revealed over the issue of what type of government the newly independent countries should have. Large numbers of Creoles wanted independence under a king—Iturbide and San Martín are the best examples. Even though Bolívar advocated a republican form of government, it was to be a conservative form of republicanism. Bolívar wanted a lifetime president with the power to appoint his own successor.

Admiration for the U.S. System and Why It Didn't Work in Nineteenth-Century Spanish America

The Spanish American creoles admired the United States' example of revolution. Many Spanish American countries admired the United States so much that they adopted our constitution almost word for word. This may be amazing for us to contemplate at a time when U.S. moral influence in the world has fallen so low. But Latin American countries could not make these constitutions work in the nineteenth century, when the United States could. This was not because "Americans" were somehow "smarter" than Spanish Americans but is rooted in historical reasons. Quite simply, American aristocrats like Washington and Jefferson had a great deal of experience in writing their own laws and conducting their own affairs under the colonial legislatures in all thirteen colonies. The Creoles who took over in Spanish America were barred from such experience by Spain. All laws were written in Spain, and Creoles were barred from offices that would have given them experience in running their own affairs.

Therefore, it was not until well into the twentieth century that many Spanish American countries acquired the political experience to make democracy work. However, it is great cause for optimism that today every country in the Western Hemisphere is a democracy, except for Castro's Cuba.

The Spanish American Social Pyramid after the Revolutions for Independence

Questions for Reflection and Review

1. Who were the Spanish American creoles? How important was their role in the independence of Spanish America from Spain? What social group did the Creoles resent the most and which social group did they fear? What type of revolution did the Creoles "decide" to have?

_____

_____

_____

_____

_____

_____

2. The Spanish empire lasted from 1492 to about 1825. How did it stay together for so long? In your opinion, how successful were the Spanish in imprinting their religion, culture, and language on Spanish America? What was the event in Spain that sparked the beginnings of independence? Why did the Spanish empire in America finally fall apart?

_____

_____

_____

_____

_____

_____

3. The Spanish Americans greatly admired the United States' revolution and its system of government. In fact, many newly free Latin American republics attempted to duplicate the American system of government in the nineteenth century but failed. Why was the United States able to "hit the ground running" with the democratic system, while it took Latin America well into the twentieth century to do so? In other words, what historical differences in the background of the United States and the background in Spanish America aided or impeded democracy?

_____

_____

_____

_____

_____

Conclusion
Four Revolutions Compared

A Small World: How the Spark of Revolution Transformed Two Continents in Only Fifty Years

The period 1775 to 1825 saw a remarkable series of four revolutions that would forever change the history of the world in the space of only fifty years. All four revolutions were intimately connected; indeed, some men personally fought in more than one of them. The American, French, Haitian, and Spanish American revolutions were mutually interactive—that is, they continued to affect each other in a continuous loop. Thus, the American Revolution didn't just end and give way to the French; rather, the French Revolution set off a series of events leading to the Haitian Revolution, which in turn had major repercussions in Spanish America and the United States.

Two Political and Two Social Revolutions

The major thesis of this book is that the four revolutions broke down into two distinctive varieties: social and political. Nobody will dispute that the French and Haitian revolutions were social revolutions by any definition. The French revolution toppled the old order and destroyed forever the basis of power of the nobles and the Church. The king of France and many of the nobles were literally eliminated by beheading, and the church was symbolically beheaded with the power of the pope being transferred to control of the French nation over its church. The Parisian mob and the lower and middle orders were enshrined in leadership in the personages of Danton and Robespierre. The French Revolution sought to reinvent the world, changing the calendar, the system of measurement, and even attempting to install a new civil religion.

In Haiti the French were slaughtered man, woman, and child in the uprising known as the Night of Fire, led by the Voodoo priest Boukman. French control of the island was forever lost under the inspiring leadership of the ex-slave Toussaint

L'ouverture. This was the only example in history of a slave society successfully throwing off a European mother country, and it inspired slaves everywhere while terrifying U.S. slave holders, European colonialists, and Spanish American Creoles.

The concept that the American Revolution was a political and not a social one may be more controversial. Certainly prominent historians such as Gordon Wood have argued the opposite. But in order to sustain his thesis, Wood has to extend the period covered by *The Radicalism of the American Revolution* well into the 1840s, whereas my analysis examines events as they were in the 1820s.

It is true that the concept of democracy itself is a radical one. The only previous successful democratic experiment lasted a little more than a century in classical Athens and some other Greek city-states. Historians tend to dismiss the Roman Republic as a true experiment in democracy because, despite its name, the Roman Republic was so corrupted that the ideal of democracy was not realized.

I would contend that in a true social revolution, there must be some inversion of the social pyramid—that is, some groups must rise from the bottom of the pyramid. Did that really happen in the American Revolution? I do not believe so. Rather, King George was replaced by American aristocrats—George Washington, Thomas Jefferson, and John Adams, to name a few. Sam Adams, who could be seen as the Robespierre of the American Revolution, did not lead the nation. Thus, the American Revolution is captured perfectly in the title of Bernard Bailyn's book, *A Struggle for Power,* for the revolution was surely a battle over whether English aristocrats or American aristocrats would rule.

The tinge of social revolution, which seems to adhere to the American Revolution in retrospect, is a result of what I call the "Onward and Upward School" of American historiography. To lay out the "Onward and Upward" viewpoint briefly: It all started with the Magna Carta. The Magna Carta was the first limitation on the power of the king. Then the Mayflower Compact, with its ideas of democracy in church government, foreshadowed the concept of a democratic system for the whole country. The Revolution then brought about political independence, and then the Civil War freed the slaves. American women received the right to vote in the early twentieth century, and blacks received full citizenship due to the civil rights struggles of the 1950s and 1960s and *Brown v. Board of Education.* Someday, gay Americans will receive their equal rights (in my opinion those who oppose gay rights today will in the future be judged in the same way that those who opposed racial integration are today). The political revolution in America certainly set the stage for eventual social progress, but it did not bring it for many years.

In fact, the adoption of the Constitution and the abandonment of the Articles of Confederation as the American form of government can be seen as a conservative triumph and confirmation that "gentlemen," and not the average man, would be in charge of the nation. Aspects of the Constitution, such as the Electoral College, moved control of the government further away from the will of the people. The framers of the Constitution simply did not trust the people to run the government and thus constructed an effective barrier to control by the people. The anachronism of the Electoral College (and meddling by the Supreme Court) gave us George W. Bush as president in 2001 even though Al Gore received a half-million more votes. The authors of the Constitution did not trust the average man, let alone women, blacks, and Indians. I am not arguing that the Articles were a better form of government than the Constitution, just that this form was closer to the people.

Minority groups and women have now mostly attained their rights in this country, but not as a direct result of the American Revolution. To give just one example, it took the Civil War to end slavery. Equality came about slowly and painfully. The first real move toward equality came with Andrew Jackson and his exaltation of the "common man." One textbook I used to assign included a chapter on Jackson titled, exactly and correctly, as "The Triumph of the White Man's Democracy." The American Revolution was a political revolution *only;* social change was a long time coming.

The American Revolution as First Cause

The American example of rule without a king was enormously influential in Europe and the rest of America. It fit in well with the Enlightenment view of the world as a place that operated according to logical laws. There was no need for a king if men were inherently rational. Yet even the French Enlightenment writers did not envision a government run by average people, and certainly not by women. Voltaire called for an "enlightened despotism," and Montesquieu would have retained a king with his powers "balanced" by other branches of the government. The French Revolution started exactly as the American had, as a dispute over taxation. At first the revolutionaries seemed intent on making only small limitations on the king's power, but soon the revolt spun out of control and ended up as a bloody and thoroughgoing social revolution. The French revolutionaries eventually decided to burn down the barn to rid it of rats. It was truly radicalism run amok, as eventually the concept was to level Old France and create an entirely new edifice.

▲ Revolution among Frenchmen and French Colonists—Social Upheavals

Why were the Americans able to limit their revolution to a changing of the political guard, while the French ended up wrecking the entire old structure of France? Surely the reasons are extremely complex, but I will attempt two main hypotheses. First, Americans simply had to rid themselves of what they had come to perceive as "foreign domination." The king of England lived across the Atlantic Ocean, and when his agents, in the person of the British Army, were defeated, so was he. Louis XVI was no foreign despot, although some liked to argue that his wife was a foreign contagion.

Another reason that the French Revolution crossed over from a political to a bloody social revolution was the character of Louis XVI himself. To call Louis indecisive is an understatement. He did not wish to anger the French people, but on the other hand, he had no desire to give up any royal prerogatives. His most crucial mistake was probably giving in through intimidation to the Third Estate receiving equal representation with the other two estates. That decision, coupled with the fact that liberal members of the first two estates sided with the Third, was crucial in launching a revolution instead of a simple meeting to determine how France would meet its debt problems. Still, a more decisive man than Louis XVI might have ended up with no worse than a constitutionally limited monarchy and his head still attached.

The difference in religious traditions in the United States and France may be another reason that the Americans ended up with a political revolution and the French a social one. The United States was founded upon, among other principles, the desire of people to be able to practice their own religions without hindrance. The diversity of American beliefs caused our founding fathers to treat the issue of religion with extreme caution. Indeed there is no more clear reflection of this than the beautifully simple and concise wording of the First Amendment to the Constitution, which prohibits the government from establishing a religion and also prohibits government interference with the free practice of religion by the citizens. Separation of church and state has served this nation well. Some recent political leaders would do well to ponder this as they try to blur the line between church and state in America.

In France, there was no separation of church and state. Since the revocation of the Edict on Nantes, France had been declared a Catholic country. Churchmen such as Cardinal Richelieu and Cardinal Mazarin often effectively ran the country. In fact, the United States is unique among the four revolutions in being a multi-religious country. Spanish America was Catholic. Even though Voodoo was equally as important in Haiti as Catholicism, it was not thought of as in opposition to Catholicism, but rather as blended in a syncretic manner with it. Thus, to demolish the edifice of Old France, one of its pillars, Catholicism, must be attacked. The conflicts between anti-clericals and defenders of the Church both in France and Spanish America absorbed a lot of energy that could have more profitably been used to solve other pressing problems. In France anti-Catholicism cost the revolution the support of conservatively religious peasants, who otherwise agreed with the ideals of the revolution. The lack of anti-clericalism in the Haitian Revolution may be attributed to the devoutness of its leader, Toussaint, and the support of the revolution by many of the clergy in Haiti.

Once the Paris mob was convinced of the treason of the king, symbolized by his attempt to flee the country, believers in limited monarchy, such as Lafayette, were also discredited. Once the king was executed, the question shifted to what type of government France should have. The model became the United States, a democratic republic. The early concepts of French democracy seemed to echo practices that had worked in America. For instance, the division between "active citizens" and "passive citizens" mirrored property qualifications for voting in the United States.

The United States had historical precedents that allowed it to channel its energies into a political revolution. The fact that Americans had been writing their own laws since the House of Burgesses and that every colony had a similar assembly, gave the fledgling country a head start on a new political system. On the other hand, France had been run by absolute kings. There was no training for self-government. The Estates General, the closest institution to the British Parliament, had not been called in for more than 150 years. Given this lack of background, it is not surprising that French attempts at democracy were abortive. When the inevitable reaction to the Terror set in, the Directory annulled or ignored elections time and time again.

Also unique in the French situation was the number of external enemies France had. Austria, Prussia, Russia, and England, alone or in some combination, set out to "do in" the Revolution. There is an old saying that you're not paranoid if they really are out to get you. France had genuine and multiple outside enemies. The fact that France seemed beset both by internal and external enemies goes far in explaining, if not condoning, the Reign of Terror. Again, the Americans were fortunate in having to only overcome one enemy, England. The other European countries, especially France, contributed money and men, if only to get back at the English for losses in the French and Indian wars. Material aid to America, in turn, made the French financial situation worse.

The French Revolution was a genuine social revolution. The king and many nobles had been beheaded, the church cowed, many archaic feudal fees no longer had to be paid by the peasants, and titles of nobility had been abolished. Men of the middle and lower classes came into true power. There are no equivalents of Robespierre and Toussaint in the American and Spanish American Revolutions, simply because they were not social revolutions.

The French Revolution had profound political implications in the United States. In fact our two original political parties, the Federalists and the Republicans, took opposite sides on the question of the French Revolution. Jefferson and the Republicans favored the revolution, while Hamilton and the Federalists deplored it. One worldwide result of the French Revolution is the use of the political terms *left* and *right,* which grew out of the tendency of the more radical French politicians to sit on the left side of the Assembly while the more conservative members sat on the right.

The French Revolution could not help but affect affairs in France's colony of St. Dominique. Only the most radical Frenchmen supported ending slavery in Haiti, and none supported Haiti's independence. Even the Society of the Friends of the Blacks would have settled for an amelioration of slave conditions, if slavery could not be abolished.

Among the many Haitian observers present in France during the Revolution, the mulatto Vincent Ogé interpreted acts of the French Assembly as giving the vote to mulattoes in Haiti. But when Ogé tried to enforce the newly proclaimed rights in Haiti, the white power structure had him summarily executed in a particularly bloody way to make an example of anyone who would interfere with the wildly profitable Haitian colonial system.

The value of Haiti's agricultural products, particularly sugar, was hugely important to a France that had gone into a revolutionary convulsion, originally set off by a huge national debt. By some accounts, Haiti provided more than 30 percent of France's revenue. Ideas of "liberty, equality, and fraternity" could not be allowed to interfere with that bottom line.

An uprising led by the Voodoo priest Boukman culminated in the Night of Fire in which many whites were killed and their plantations ravaged in northern Haiti. The future leader of Haiti, the ex-slave Toussaint L'ouverture, made sure that his master and master's family were safely away before he joined the slave rebellion. Toussaint's treatment of his former master was only a foreshadowing of his far-sighted policy of racial tolerance.

Toussaint is wrongly undervalued by history. Here was an ex-slave who was virtually self-taught, with a little help from a priest. Toussaint outmaneuvered and outfought the Spanish and English who tried to take advantage of the French Revolution and would have retained slavery. He even managed to take over the whole island of Hispaniola when the odds would have favored the Spanish and the English to do so. Toussaint was astute at navigating the treacherous crosscurrents of internal Haitian politics, playing off the mulattoes versus the French, the Jacobins versus the monarchists, and any number of other combinations of political forces.

Toussaint was a self-taught military genius. He mastered the art of hit-and-run and guerrilla tactics. He defeated French, Spanish, and English regular troops. Although France spared no effort to retake Haiti, it could never undo the revolution that Toussaint had wrought. Nor could any other European power reintroduce slavery. This was a true social revolution. The social pyramid completely inverted and blacks came out on top. Even the largest invasion force sent overseas by France under Napoleon's brother-in-law could not reverse Haiti's social revolution. Only Toussaint's desire to maintain some type of commonwealth status under France and French underhandedness finally landed him in a French prison. Nevertheless, the revolution was safe.

In a profoundly racist world, Toussaint was perceived as a major threat by the European and American social order. And yet he would not allow the Haitian Revolution to veer off into racial vindictiveness and revenge. He insisted that Haiti needed all its citizens, black, white, and mulatto. This was the most enlightened racial policy of its time in the world. Toussaint was also correct about the need to maintain the large plantations as the basis of Haiti's wealth and the expertise of the white planters to run them. How much better off Haiti might be today had the first black president, Dessalines, and the first mulatto president, Pétion, followed Toussaint's racial and economic policies.

The glory of the Haitian Revolution has been overshadowed by subsequent events on that unhappy island. Conflicts between mulattoes and blacks, environmental damage cause by deforestation, and vindictive boycotts, embargoes, blockades, and foreign interventions have all taken their toll on Haiti. Among the most recent was the invasion and occupation by the United States from 1915 to 1934, with no legitimate rationale behind it.

The Haitian Revolution was fully as important as any of the other three that occurred in the late eighteenth and early nineteenth centuries. It indirectly allowed the United States to double its territory, when Napoleon, disillusioned by his defeat in Haiti, decided that Louisiana was expendable. The Haitian Revolution frightened slave holders around the world and caused American slave owners to hold their slaves ever tighter. Ironically, in this sense, the Haitian Revolution may have made the lot of slaves elsewhere harder.

Haiti did attempt to export its revolution, though not in the way Europeans originally feared (directly instigating slave revolts in other Caribbean islands). Instead, Haiti armed and funded Spanish American revolutions with the hope that slavery would be banished from those newly independent lands. This promise of the Haitian Revolution was rapidly fulfilled.

▲ Spanish America—an Admiration for the American System without the Background for Democracy

Grateful as they were for Haitian aid, the Creoles who led the Spanish American revolutions were not about to let a social revolution occur in México and Central and South America. The only chance of this happening in Spanish America died with Father Hidalgo. We can only theorize what type of country México might have become in the early nineteenth century, had Father Hidalgo not hesitated to loose his hordes on México City.

The man who eventually brought independence to México, Augustín de Iturbide, had no thoughts of social reform. His was to be strictly a political revolution, which replaced Ferdinand VII with Augustín I, Emperor of México, for a short time. Though the Creoles who overthrew Augustín changed México's form of government to a republic, they had no intent of extending the politically active portion of the Mexican citizenry much past the upper 20 percent of the population. The Liberals would let a few more upwardly mobile mestizos into power than the Conservatives would.

México in the first half of the nineteenth century was dominated by the *caudillo* (strong man on horseback) Antonio Lopez de Santa Anna. While giving lip service to first liberal, then conservative ideals, Santa Anna's only true cause was Santa Anna. México simply lacked the historical background and education to make a republican form of government work at that time.

The Conservative Party in México displayed its folly by sponsoring an Austrian prince, Maximilian, as king of México. (The United States could not intervene under the Monroe Doctrine to throw the Europeans out, since they were involved in the Civil War at the time.) The Liberal Party with the full-blooded Indian president, Benito Juárez, drove out the French but unfortunately squandered important time and goodwill with ill-conceived attacks on the Catholic Church. México would have to wait until 1910 for a true social revolution to break out.

The South American Creoles may have been split on what type of government to install after independence, but they agreed that there should be no social revolution with its possibility of Indian revolt. Bolívar favored a republican form of government with a very strong executive, while San Martín favored a constitutional monarchy. Both major Spanish American leaders, however, agreed that Creoles must be firmly in control.

The Four Revolutions and Their Influence on Later Revolutions

The Spanish American Revolution brought the first Age of Revolutions full circle, with an American-style political revolution. Although the Spanish Americans attempted to copy the U.S. federal republican system, they were unable to successfully do so in the nineteenth century, due to a lack of experience in running their own affairs.

Other historians, most notably Crane Brinton with his 1938 classic *The Anatomy of Revolution,* have written on comparative revolutions and attempted to classify them as to type. Brinton compares the English, French, American, and Russian revolutions. The four that interested me were the American, French, Haitian, and Spanish American revolutions. They all occurred within the short span of fifty years, and all profoundly affected each other. Some men actually fought in more than one of these revolutions. By now the reader knows that I consider the Haitian Revolution equally as important as the other three—and wrongly neglected. As for the Russian Revolution, I would compare it with the Mexican Revolution of 1910.

I hope that this short volume has whetted the reader's appetite to delve further into this fascinating fifty-year period spanning four revolutions. I know that not everyone will agree with my conclusions, but I hope the framework I have presented will stimulate discussion and interest in a truly fascinating, and not that distant, period of history.

Index

CPSIA information can be obtained
at www.ICGtesting.com
Printed in the USA
LVHW020710240722
724122LV00002B/3